Foreword

The Salvation Army is nothing if not evangelistic. It is in our DNA—it is who we are. Once we have affirmed a faith in Jesus Christ and accepted Him as our Savior, our "common aim is to induce others to subject themselves to the lordship of Christ" (*Chosen to Be a Soldier*).

Since 1968, The Salvation Army in the United States has conducted a National Seminar on Evangelism at the Navigator's Glen Eyrie Conference Center in Colorado Springs, Colorado. This annual event has provided inspiration and instruction in the lifestyle of the Salvationist-Evangelist, and opportunities to review ways to stimulate interest and commitment to soul saving efforts.

What follows here are first-person accounts representative of nearly 5400 delegates and 900 staff members who have participated in the seminar. These are true stories with life changing consequences.

We are grateful to Lt. Colonel Stephen Banfield, National Secretary for Program, and Major Donna Leedom, Assistant National Secretary for Program, at National Headquarters, for undertaking this effort, and especially to those who contributed by sharing of themselves. We have heard the story and will be the better for it.

As preparations were underway for the 1968 event, it was prayed that "the blessing of our Heavenly Father would be on the decision reached,

Foreword

and that the result would be outstanding advances in our soul saving and soldier making efforts."

I believe a reading of what follows will confirm that that prayer has indeed been heard, and more than abundantly answered.

Commissioner William A. Roberts
USA National Commander

SAY SOME THING

TELL THEM. WIN THEM. ESTABLISH THEM.

INSPIRING ACCOUNTS OF EVERYDAY EVANGELISM

By Stephen Banfield and Donna Leedom

Foreword by Commissioner William A. Roberts

CREST BOOKS

Salvation Army National Headquarters
Alexandria, VA, USA

Copyright © 2013 by The Salvation Army

First Reprint 2013

Published by Crest Books
The Salvation Army National Headquarters
615 Slaters Lane
Alexandria, VA 22313

Phone: 703/684-5523
Fax: 703/302-8617

Major Allen Satterlee, Editor in Chief and National Literary Secretary
Judith L. Brown, Crest Books Editor
Roger Selvage, Art Director
Henry Cao, Graphic Designer

Available from The Salvation Army Supplies and Purchasing Departments
        Des Plaines, IL—(847) 937-8896
        West Nyack, NY—(888) 488-4882
        Atlanta, GA—(800) 786-7372
        Long Beach, CA—(847) 937-8896

Also visit shop.salvationarmy.org

Printed in the United States of America

ISBN: 978-0-9831482-8-9
Library of Congress Control Number: 2013933278

Contents

Keep the flag up
wear your uniform
and say something
to some poor sinner
every day and you
will not go far
astray.

William Booth
April 1911.

"Keep the flag up, wear your uniform and <u>say something</u> to some poor sinner every day and you will not go far astray."

William Booth
April 1911

Preface

"As the rain and the snow come down from heaven, and do not return to it without watering the earth so that it yields seed for the sower and bread for the eater,

So is my word that goes out from my mouth:

It will not return to me empty, but will accomplish what I desire and achieve the purpose for which I sent it" (Isaiah 55:10-11).

The gospel is shared by those serving in The Salvation Army in two very important ways—proclamation and demonstration. We have no trouble at all demonstrating the grace of Jesus Christ in times of need or crisis. We serve meals, provide shelter, visit the lonely, listen to the desperate, comfort the grieving, and offer safety in the storm as the hands of Christ to those in need. We are experts in the demonstration of the gospel, epitomizing the words of Saint Francis of Assisi, "Preach the gospel at all times, if necessary use words."

But dear ones, words are necessary. Proclamation of the gospel is what gives clarity to its demonstration. Words are important, so we must *Say Something*. Each year at the National Seminar on Evangelism, soldiers and officers come to Glen Eyrie in Colorado Springs, Colorado, to give time and attention to the proclamation of the gospel. So many have come with the notion that evangelism is a gift, one they do not possess. It is a gift. Truly there are those in our ranks with a God-given ability to turn every conversation toward eternity. But evangelism is also the responsibility of every believer. The good news is that God is not only the giver of the gift. He is able to equip each of us to do the work of an evangelist, and to provide what is needed to accomplish His desired outcome.

God does not expect us to save the world. That is His work, completed in the life, death and resurrection of Jesus Christ. We are His obedient and faithful witnesses. After we have seen His wondrous work, heard the gospel of grace and power and known the renewing and guidance of the Holy Spirit, we only need the opportunity to share God's story and the difference it has made in our lives. We are called to grow sensitive and attentive to the Spirit, to learn more about God's story and to understand our own, so that when God nudges us we will be ready to *Say Something*, as a witness to His mercy and love.

In this book, stories of those who have attended the Salvation Army's National Seminar on Evangelism are captured to inspire and encourage you. They represent the witness of soldiers and officers in every territory, in corps large and small. Perhaps you will see something of yourself and your situation in the pages that follow. These are real people, with real doubts in their abilities, with real fear of rejection and ridicule, but with REAL faith in God. It is our hope that you will take note of the "failures" as much as the triumphs. It is important to remember that simply because our words haven't led to a confession of faith doesn't mean they didn't accomplish God's desired purpose. Deepening dependence on the Holy Spirit and ready obedience will bring the harvest God has in mind. We only need to be courageous enough to depend on Him in the proclamation of the gospel, in the way we have come to depend on Him in its demonstration.

Also included in this book are photos taken of the Glen Eyrie grounds. The natural beauty of this place has invited those who have attended NSE to "join with all nature in manifold witness" to God's character and desire for reconciliation. It is our hope in including them to offer a glimpse into this part of the NSE experience, and to invite you to celebrate, with all creation, our great God of faithfulness, mercy and love.

It's time to share the gospel in its entirety . . . proclamation and demonstration. Let's "*Say Something* to some poor sinner every day, and (we) will not go far astray."

Chapter *One*

How It All Started

When Salvationists don their uniforms, The Salvation Army's mission is communicated by the prominent "S's" on the uniform lapels. While we have been comfortable in declaring that they stand for "Saved to Serve," the original intention was to be a constant reminder that we are "Saved to Save." When a Salvation Army soldier is enrolled, the Soldier's Covenant begins by declaring one's own salvation experience "having accepted Jesus Christ as my Savior and Lord." This is followed by the promise to "be faithful to the purposes for which God raised up The Salvation Army, sharing the good news of Jesus Christ, endeavoring to win others to Him." In fact, this charge to witness as Salvationists is evidenced through the youngest Junior Soldiers, who, in innocence of faith, recite a similar Promise that says, "Having asked God for forgiveness . . . I will try to help others follow Him."

Evangelism is the ethos of The Salvation Army. We stand in the gap as a saved people whose primary purpose is to reconcile sinful, separated humanity with a sinless loving Divinity through the atoning death of Jesus Christ. We serve a loving, forgiving God who "demonstrates His own love for us in this: While we were still sinners, Christ died for us" (Romans 5:8). While our service to humanity is a response from our own salvation experience, it cannot save us or other sinners. It is the salvific work of Christ alone which reconciles man to his Maker. The evangelistic passion of the Salvationist is insatiable and must remain so. To that end we of the Army must always be aware of the changing world around us and the compelling message within us.

The National Seminar on Evangelism was born out of the need of the times and an incessant desire to introduce people to Christ. In the United States the decade of the 1960's was a time of rampant promiscuity, rebellion against traditional institutions, the hippie movement, and the waging of the divisive Vietnam War, which left more than 58,000 dead and another 150,000 wounded. The minds and hearts of society were in turmoil, hopelessness and disbelief. No longer could preachers "preach people into the Kingdom." The use of canned evangelism programs was ineffective. Methods had to change. Principles remained immutable, but methods had to change.

As early as 1957, the establishment of a National Evangelism Commission was raised; however, the effectively functioning territorial evangelism commissions appeared to obviate the need to create a national body. The establishment of a national commission received periodic review, until in 1963 the NEC was formed to plan the evangelistic crusade for The Salvation Army's Centenary celebration in 1965. The success of these plans resulted in the September 1966 Commissioners' Conference approving the recommendation "that, in view of the expressed concern of Salvationists of all levels in the Second Century of our history, the National Evangelism Commission be established as a permanent commission to meet at regular intervals." The membership of this first commission included the following:

Central:	**Captain William Himes**	
	Corps Sergeant-Major Frank Staiger	
East:	**Lt. Colonel John D. Waldron**	
	B/M Alfred Swenarton	
South:	**Mrs. Major Byrd Hudson**	
	Young Peoples' Sergeant-Major Milton Servais	
West:	**Major Herbert Wiseman**	
	Corps Sergeant-Major Jack K. Wood	

Sensing a need to reaffirm their commitment to evangelism, the soldiers of the National Evangelism Commission issued a signed manifesto, which read:

> "Evangelism is the presentation of Christ Jesus in the power of the Holy Spirit, urging men to place their trust in God, accept the new life Christ offers as Savior, and serve Him as Lord in this world in the fellowship of His church."
>
> In a world of changing cultures, societies and methods, there remain the basics that never change; human nature, the Gospel and the Holy Spirit, who is the agent of divine communication. The Person of Jesus Christ is still the answer to the deepest needs of mankind, and man's only hope of redemption.
>
> The Apostles of old were so Christ-centered in their living that the people "took knowledge that they had been with Jesus." They thought as He did, they showed love as He did, and they felt compassion for the suffering and lost of their generation. Because evangelism cares, it cannot pass by human misery.
>
> With renewed vigor and dedication to God and The Salvation Army, we must use every means to reach this generation for Jesus Christ.
>
> We, the soldiers of the "National Evangelism Commission" call every Salvationist to full time service as a "personal evangelist" in the spirit and tradition of the layman apostles who founded the first-century church. It is our divine privilege to

TELL THEM • WIN THEM • ESTABLISH THEM

> The goal is before us. The resources for fulfilling our task, as revealed in God's Word, are available. Let us individually pray with the apostle Paul. "Lord, what will you have me to do?" and then in partnership with the Holy Spirit—do it!

vangelism is the presentation of Christ Jesus in the power of the Holy Spirit, urging men to place their trust in God, accept the new life Christ offers as Saviour, and serve Him as Lord in this world in the fellowship of His church."

In a world of changing cultures, societies and methods, there remain the basics that never change; human nature, the Gospel and the Holy Spirit, who is the agent of divine communication. The Person of Jesus Christ is still the answer to the deepest needs of mankind; and man's only hope of redemption.

The Apostles of old were so Christ-centered in their living that the people "took knowledge that they had been with Jesus." They thought as He did, they showed love as He did, and they felt compassion for the suffering and lost of their generation. Because evangelism cares, it cannot pass by human misery.

With renewed vigor and dedication to God and The Salvation Army, we must use every means to reach this generation for Jesus Christ.

We, the soldiers of the "National Evangelism Commission" call every Salvationist to full time service as a "personal evangelist" in the spirit and tradition of the layman apostles who founded the first-century church. It is our divine privilege to

Tell them ❦ Win them ❦ Establish them

The goal is before us. The resources for fulfilling our task, as revealed in God's Word, are available. Let us individually pray with the apostle Paul, "Lord, what will you have me to do?" and then in partnership with the Holy Spirit—do it!

Jack K. Wood

CORPS SERGEANT-MAJOR
LOS ANGELES, CALIFORNIA, TABERNACLE CORPS

Alfred V. Swenarton

BANDMASTER
ASBURY PARK, NEW JERSEY, CITADEL CORPS

Frank O. Staiger

CORPS SERGEANT-MAJOR
PORT HURON, MICHIGAN, CORPS

Milton Servais

YOUNG PEOPLE'S SERGEANT-MAJOR
NASHVILLE, TENNESSEE, CORPS

The prayerful discussions and planning of the National Evangelism Commission in September 1966 produced a recommendation to the Commissioners' Conference (CC) which read in part, "That, in view of the need of Salvationists for a shared experience in the art of mass and personal evangelism, a 'Laymen's National Institute on Evangelism' be immediately established. That this Institute be convened in the summer of 1967."

In response, the Commissioners' Conference (CC), chaired by National Commander, Commissioner Samuel Hepburn, "recognized the recommendations have real merit." Wise counsel and direction was given by the Army leaders, and official CC minutes indicate they "earnestly prayed that the blessing of our Heavenly Father would be upon the decisions reached, and the result would be outstanding advances in our soul-saving and soldier-making efforts" [Sept.–Oct. 1966 CC Minutes]. With official approval granted, the planning stage began. Planning for any inaugural event usually takes more time and effort than originally thought. The Laymen's National Institute on Evangelism was no exception. A lengthy planning session for the National Evangelism Commission, held in Chicago, Illinois, January 31– February 4, 1967, recognized a shortage of time to organize this event for July 1967, as previously hoped. The new date recommended to the Commissioners' Conference was July 22-26, 1968. The location selected for the Institute was the Navigators' Conference Center at Glen Eyrie, located in picturesque Colorado Springs, Colorado. Green Lake, Wisconsin and Winona Lake, Indiana were also considered, with the latter being considered for 1969 and 1970.

The delay of the inaugural Laymen's National Institute on Evangelism meant that the Institute did not happen … at least not under that name! The Commissioners' Conference was in the process of renaming the "Laymen's Commission" to become "The Salvation Army Soldiers' Commission," hence the Institute became "The Salvation Army Soldiers' National Institute on Evangelism" (May 1967 CC Minutes). The use of the term "institute" appeared to be short-lived when the name was again changed to "The Salvation Army Soldiers' National Seminar on Evangelism" (February 1968 CC Minutes). Three names before the seminar ever began!

How It All Started

The faculty assigned for the 1968 Soldiers' National Seminar on Evangelism included:

Commissioner Samuel Hepburn	National Commander
Commissioner Edward Carey	Eastern Territory
Colonel Emil Nelson	National Headquarters
Colonel Bramwell Tripp	Central Territory
Lt. Colonel Max Kurtz	Western Territory
Lt. Colonel John D. Waldron	Eastern Territory
Brigadier Victor Newbould	Western Territory
Major Ernest Miller	Central Territory
Captain Paul Marshall	Central Territory
Other presenters included:	
Captain Bramwell Tillsley	Bible Study Teacher
Lt. Colonel Lyell Rader	Outdoor Evangelism
Major Ernest Miller	Music Evangelism
Captain David Baxendale	Teen Evangelism
Lt. Colonel Charles Talmadge	Follow-up Evangelism
Major William Himes	Contemporary Evangelism
Captain Harold J. Anderson	Singspiration leader
Mr. Lorne Sanny	The Navigators

Major Shirley Sipley was appointed to assume clerical duties and to serve as the seminar pianist. Other support staff lectured and led various activities.

In hindsight, we discover an ironic note in the selection process for the NSE faculty, which was directed by then Lt. Colonel Waldron. The Colonel wanted to hold a United Bible class each morning for all of the delegates. He had no trouble filling the other staff positions, but he had been unable to decide who should lead the Bible class. One of the suggestions was Captain Bramwell Tillsley of Canada. Initially, the Colonel would not even consider Captain Tillsley as a candidate. "We cannot trust this most important assignment to an unknown captain," he said. After a thorough search was conducted, Captain Tillsley was again recommended to lead the Bible study. Colonel Waldron then reluctantly agreed. Captain Tillsley would go on to serve as the international leader of The Salvation Army from 1993–1994!

On July 27, 1968, the National Evangelism Commission met following the seminar to discuss its benefits and challenges. Previous planning meetings had involved discussion that seminars in 1969 and 1970 might be held at either Winona Lake or Green Lake, Indiana. A survey of the delegates and Commission members revealed almost a unanimous desire to remain at Glen Eyrie for all future seminars. The minutes of the Commission's meeting stated that, "the spirit and dedication of the Glen Eyrie staff, the grounds, atmosphere, suitable accommodations, and central location all lend themselves to make Glen Eyrie an ideal setting for this type of seminar."

1968 NSE—THE WAR CRY ARTICLE
FOR SEPTEMBER 14, 1968

"Evangelism—Their Prior Task"

At the first Soldiers' National Seminar on Evangelism held at Glen Eyrie, The Navigators' conference grounds at Colorado Springs, 90 male and 30 female Salvationists surveyed the Army's supreme task. Having agreed that the open-air ministry is entering on a new and effective phase of usefulness, they discussed the four classical methods and then went to park and pavement to test their convictions. In the park, where many hippies were gathered, they proved that personal encounters with bystanders were most effective.

The National Commander, Commissioner Samuel Hepburn, and the Eastern Territorial Commander, Commissioner Edward Carey, headed a staff that kept the horizons wide and drew all discussions back to Bible sources. Among the delegates were an insurance salesman, a physicist engaged in advanced research, a political officeholder, housewives, social and group workers, business and professional men, and one from skid row, who has spent years in evangelism. White and black members of integrated Army corps shared experiences and observations. One, who is now doing visitation and other groundwork for an Army center in a ghetto, spoke of the need to be "real" and "mean business" in order to reach people.

How It All Started

In 1969, the NEC launched a program to reinforce the soldiers' efforts to share the Gospel. The following eyewitness account describes the successful second year of that program.

THE SOLDIERS' NATIONAL SEMINAR ON EVANGELISM—1969

At the time the National Evangelism Commission issued the manifesto that appears on another page, it became evident that some definite and constructive means should be made available to inspire and instruct soldiers in the art of personal witnessing and winning others to Christ.

The National Evangelism Commission recommended to the Commissioners' Conference of The Salvation Army in the United States, that a Soldiers' Seminar in Evangelism be established for this purpose. Permission was gladly given and the NEC proceeded to develop a program.

The first session met in July 1968, at the Navigators, Glen Eyrie, Colorado Springs, Colorado.

As soldiers gathered from all over the United States and Canada, they became comrades in arms at first sight, and the unity of the Spirit of Christ was made known in every contact and conversation.

During the year that has passed, numerous letters and verbal expressions have proven the effectiveness and lasting value of the seminar.

Soldiers returned to their corps with renewed zeal and enthusiasm for their basic responsibility to be personal witnesses and workers. A new respect for and faith in the ministry of The Salvation Army became apparent, and soldiers found a new dimension of their own value in the movement dedicated to win others for Christ.

With such a beginning, the Commissioners' Conference has again given approval for the seminar to be held.

Let every delegate, faculty and staff member join in private and public prayer that the seminar will be a source of spiritual growth, new enthusiasm and renewed dedication to God and His work in and through The Salvation Army.

Respectfully submitted by Mrs. James (Evelyn) Smith, Secretary

The next significant change in the Soldiers' National Seminar on Evangelism occurred in 1992. For many years concern had been voiced that soldier delegates to the seminar had returned to their own corps "on fire for the Lord," but that the enthusiasm soon died out because corps officers lacked the same experience and the same passion. It was not necessarily a matter of will, but rather of practical knowledge—not having been there with their soldiers, corps officers were missing the frame of reference that had engendered emotional intensity. The simple solution was for corps officers to accompany delegates, take the same classes, share the same field training and then together prayerfully develop an action plan to renew evangelism in their corps. Army leaders enthusiastically embraced this adaptation and agreed to a final name change, "National Seminar on Evangelism."

Another notable improvement occurred in 2006 when Majors Gary and Cheryl Miller, National Secretary and Associate for Program, respectively, adopted the Bill Hybels (Willow Creek Association) evangelistic plan entitled *Just Walk Across the Room.* The Millers explained the process this way:

"Just Walk Across the Room—What a novel idea in Evangelism? Who would you talk to, who would listen? These are the usual questions asked by someone given this task.

"We had arrived at NHQ and were tasked with the responsibility of finding a new and effective way to spread the gospel and then propose it to the National Seminar on Evangelism.

"Prayer and watchfulness were the primary tools to bring about a new and innovative program for the NSE delegates at their annual summer experience held in Glen Eyrie, Colorado.

"One day while on assignment Cheryl mentioned a new program idea from Willow Creek Ministries called *Just Walk Across the Room.*"

"I received a brochure in the mail from Willow Creek Church and sat down to look at what they had to offer," Major Cheryl Miller said. "I had not been to Willow Creek for many years and did not sign up to receive anything from them. So I was a little shocked when I received it.

"As I perused the brochure I really wasn't looking for anything in particular. I just wanted to see what was there. I was really just killing time reading it.

"When I came to the material *Just Walk Across the Room*, I got interested. I shared all of this with Gary and suggested that we look into it. We both read the book, watched the video, and without a shadow of a doubt we believed this was the curriculum we should use.

"We put the material together, ordered the book and video for each staff member and off we went. I grew more excited each day because I believed that brochure was sent to me for a reason. I believed God wanted that material used for Glen Eyrie. It was just perfect.

"When we presented it to the National Commander we asked for one thing—that if we chose this curriculum it would be used for at least three years. And our request was honored.

"We believe in this curriculum. We believe in the *Just Walk Across the Room* material. And we are pleased that it is still the curriculum today."

Over the years Salvationists have been criticized for their methods of evangelism, but we are doing something. One day a woman criticized the system used by the great American evangelist Dwight L. Moody to win people to the Lord. Moody's reply was, "I agree with you. I don't like the way I do it, either. Tell me, how do you do it?" The woman replied, "I don't do it." Moody retorted, "Then I like my way of doing it better than your way of not doing it."

Do something; say something!

Chapter *Two*

Don't Wait!

At the age of twelve, Robert Louis Stevenson was looking out into the dark from his upstairs window watching a man light the streetlamps. Stevenson's governess entered the room and asked what he was doing. He replied, "I am watching a man cut holes in the darkness." What an image of our task to share God's light in the darkness of this world! We are a people called and committed to cutting holes in the spiritual darkness of our world. One such person who plays an integral role in this process is Corps Sergeant Major Ken Reeves from the Greensburg, Pennsylvania corps.

Having heard from others about the blessed time they had spent at the National Seminar on Evangelism (NSE), it was Ken's hope to someday be a participant. He had received the textbook *Just Walk Across the Room* earlier as a gift, but had not read it. At NSE, however, the presentation of evangelism principles in the united sessions offered inspiration and affirmed the simplicity of sharing the gospel of Christ. It was story telling at its best and telling the best Story that exists—there is hope in Jesus Christ!

The NSE includes united sessions each day in which the four parts of Bill Hybel's book are presented. These sessions are followed by small group discussions and plans for engaging in outreach evangelism later in the week. On Thursday Ken's small group visited the Salvation Army's Adult Rehabilitation Center (ARC) in Colorado Springs. Residents of the program gathered around the dinner table to hold captivating small group discussions. (So much so that Ken missed supper!) Following the meal, the small group invited the congregation to stand, come forward and pray at the altar. It seemed like everybody went forward. At the front of the chapel people kneeled, prayed and shed tears for the poor choices they had made in life. In spite of the crowded Mercy Seat, Ken had a clear path to a young man at the altar. The scene was reminiscent of the parting of the Red Sea in that God wanted this young man to meet with Ken so that he could later claim his own salvation experience.

This young man, who was in his 30's, was drawn in by the invitation to come forward. In John 12:32, Jesus said, "And I, when I am lifted up from the earth, will draw all people to myself." The magnetism Jesus referred to was clearly evident that night. The young man had left the church, but he was hungry to know God and to experience the love of God. In his sincere search, he discovered the truth of Hebrews 11:6, " . . . anyone who comes to Him (God), must believe that He exists, and that He rewards those who earnestly seek Him."

Ken talked with this earnest seeker for more than 30 minutes, learning that he was despondent and searching for something larger than himself and his own failures. In his emptiness he even entertained the thought that God might have given up on him. But, as Ken assured him that was not the case, he opened up to the idea that God could and would love him. The notion that God was keeping hope alive even when he had lost all hope intrigued him. He was struck by the thought that even though the world sees a hopeless end, the Christian can see an endless hope in Christ. Finally, the young man came to faith in Christ. Then he gave a testimony to that act and showed a genuine change of heart. All because Ken "walked across the room" with hope to share.

After the seminar ended, Ken was waiting to catch his plane at the airport in Colorado Springs when he noticed a family, looking very despondent, standing in line. Trying not to disturb their privacy, Ken approached them and came alongside them for counsel and support. They had just attended a family funeral, and were focusing on "things above," examining their lives and their faith. Ken was prepared to share his faith, the great gift of God, which had carried him through many sad and hurting times in his own life. Ken shared the parts of his story that would help these hurting individuals know there was hope beyond the grave, not an ending but a new beginning. After offering comfort and strength, Ken boarded the plane with this grieving family. He had simply made himself available.

During a lull in the flight, an airline attendant felt drawn to Ken because of his uniform. Initially asking him what airline he was with, he, of course, took pleasure in announcing he "flies" with The Salvation Army! Then he proceeded to talk about attending the NSE in Colorado Springs and the larger work of The Salvation Army. Ken had her undivided attention for a solid 10 minutes, which is unheard of for busy flight attendants. Again, the key was genuineness and availability.

On a layover in Dallas, Ken noticed a serviceman who was eating a quick lunch at a fast food restaurant in the terminal. Initially, he thought he would just pass by, but he decided to approach the man, thanked him for his service and told him that his son is also in the military. On discovering that the soldier was bound for Iraq, Ken replied, "I have a son who is on active duty in Iraq and a Savior who is on active duty as well. The God of Abraham, Isaac and Jacob is also the God of every soldier on the field and every loving parent at home." Before they parted company, he assured the soldier that he would be praying for him and his family. The key to this encounter was to be intentional and relational.

On the final leg of his journey, Ken met an older man who was also returning home. As the conversation turned from the weather and sports to religion, Ken learned that the man's church attendance was "in limbo." Rather than focusing on membership in a certain church, Ken intentionally sought to urge his friend to consider a relationship with Christ. That mission is not always completely realized. In fact, maybe it is seldom realized, but being intentional is the key.

For Ken, evangelism is a lifestyle, not an activity that grew out of NSE. While working for many years at J.C. Penney's, he would wear a tie with Christian symbols, which opened the door for him to witness to his faith. Pointing to a Christian symbol, a customer might ask, "What does that mean?", thus offering the perfect segue to say something for the Lord. Later, as he worked in the shoe department, he always felt pleased when young people came in to purchase new shoes for their church confirmation. Ken would ask the date of the event, affirm the youth and emphasize the significance of their profession of faith.

After 20 years of employment at Penney's came to an end, lifestyle evangelism didn't! A new chapter is being written. Ken now works in the warehouse operations of Dick's Sporting Good stores. His words and his life continue to be a witness in a work environment that can get rather "rough" at times. Occasionally, a curse word will be spoken, but if Ken is present, it is usually followed by an apology, signaling that people in the secular world respect his character and spiritual integrity.

Lt. Bryan DeMichael, Ken's corps officer at the time, said of him, "One man (CSM Ken Reeves) was never the same. The passion from that event overflowed into the rest of the corps and made a tremendous impact on everyone. I would say that the NSE trip was the turning point for that corps—one that had experienced the tragic deaths of officers, tremendous internal strife and loss. I enjoyed watching my CSM (a former officer) renew his passion for evangelism and see the impact that had in the corps. It was a blessing for him to be in the same small group as Cotton Presley, who gave him even additional insight as to how to be a stronger CSM. I loved watching him interact with everyone he came in contact with on the way home, his witness and passion."

We learn some important lessons from Ken:

Be relational. God's original plan for man was to be relational. God wants us to be in community and foremost to be in community with Him. The creation story shows His master design, which in the Garden of Eden was perfect community and fellowship with Him. Man's disobedience broke that relationship and ever since God has been attempting to bring man back into relationship with his Creator. God uses His followers to tell our story, which is part of His Story, but not from a distance. He does not want us standing far off and pointing the way. No one comes to faith in Christ by our "yelling out directions" for people to go. When we come alongside and show the way through our story and God's provision for reconciliation through Jesus Christ, people are more likely to respond to and receive the claims of Christ.

Be available. Our technological age has lulled us into thinking that everything should and can come unto us. We turn a faucet and water comes to us. We hit the switch and electricity and light come to us. We sit and point a remote and the world is at our fingertips. We click a mouse and a satellite thousands of miles in the sky sends a signal down to us, and we see our backyards from outer space. The world's mantra is "Sit and it shall come unto you." Not so with evangelism. The Great Commission is recorded in

Matthew 28:19, "Therefore go and make disciples . . ." The first action verb there gives us a direct, active command, "Go." And in our going we make ourselves available. We have a distorted view of our mission, if we think we are to "sit back and they will come." CSM Cotton Presley, long time faculty member at the National Seminar on Evangelism, gives clear direction on this matter when he reminds us, "no contact, no impact."

Be intentional. Engage people for the sake of making an introduction to Christ. We do not have the right "to remain silent." Many of us are familiar with the Miranda Act, which instructs all peace officers to give the arrested party a review of his or her rights as a United States citizen. Often we hear these famous lines on television or portrayed over the radio. The one most of us remember the best is, "You have the right to remain silent; anything you say can and will be used against you in a court of law . . ." The first time we hear these words spoken, we realize the gravity of the situation. In a somewhat different way, the believer is asked a different sort of question by the Holy Spirit. We are questioned about our faith and trust in God for our eternal salvation on a daily basis by the world, and commanded to witness for the Lord in His Word.

As a recent songwriter wrote, "You don't have the right to remain silent if you have been arrested by God's grace." The truth is that we are commanded in the Bible that we do not have the right to remain silent about our faith. Christians are called to tell the world about Christ's death, resurrection, and His saving grace, and to tell of how we have been pardoned for our sins (1 Pet. 3:15). How can we then be silent about the joy of knowing Christ! Share Him with someone today! [Practical Bible Illustrations from Yesterday and Today]

Be led. Jesus is not saving the world—He has saved the world. The work of redemption has been done. Now Jesus is revealing to His children His plan of reconciling the world to himself, one person at a time. "Jesus . . . wants us to see that the neighbor next door or the people sitting next to us on a plane or in a classroom are not interruptions to our schedule. They are there by divine appointment. Jesus wants us to see their needs, their loneliness, their longings, and he wants to give us the courage to reach out to them." [Rebecca Manley Pippert]

Be expectant. Ashamedly, the Church universal has lost the sense of expectancy that fueled its fervor and zeal in earlier days. Either we have minimized our perception of the greatness of God to be able to bring people to faith in Christ, or we have maximized our perception of the depravity of man and his unwillingness to respond to the offer of forgiveness of sins. Either or both are not beyond correction! Our God is a sovereign, almighty, loving God who "so loved the world that he gave His one and only Son, that whoever believes in him shall not perish but have eternal life" (John 3:16).

Many men who have been described as some of the worst of humanity have responded to the offer of salvation ONCE IT WAS OFFERED! Expect that God is able and man is willing. As absurd as it might seem to attempt to bring Christ to a hardened person, just do it. (Thank you, NIKE.) Like the old preacher used to say, "If God tells me to jump through a stone wall, it's my responsibility to jump and it's God's responsibility to get me through!"

Stop, look and listen has always been good advice when crossing railroad tracks. However, it is also good advice when taking Christ to the world.

While all believers are given the call to evangelism, there are some who simply have received and use the spiritual gift of evangelism. One such individual known to the staff of the National Seminar on Evangelism is Paul Luhn. Paul tells the story of how just being in the neighborhood (some would call this incarnational ministry) is the first step to bringing people to Christ through bringing Christ to people.

JUST WALK DOWN THE STREET

by Paul Luhn

Right after buying a new house in a suburban neighborhood in Chicago, I decided to walk down the street and meet some of my neighbors. Two doors down was a family with two girls about the same age as my children.

I struck up a conversation with the father and listened to his story. After listening to his story I shared my story with him.

I'm not very good at home repairs, and when I found out he was a handyman and loved to help with construction projects, I knew I'd found a friend. He decided to help me fix up the house if I would tell him more about God. It wasn't long before he was hammering away in my house, putting up drywall and installing new plumbing, and I was inviting him to church and telling him about God.

A few years went by and as our relationship grew stronger, I began to feel I could not go to heaven without my new friend. God prompted me one evening to share the gospel (His story) with Tim, and I invited him out for a piece of pie at a local restaurant.

After telling Tim about God's love and the sacrifice Jesus made on his behalf, I asked him if he would like to invite Jesus into his life. His reply was, "Yes, I would. But I have one question for you. What took you so long to ask?"

That night in my car in the parking lot of that restaurant, my best friend's life changed forever as he invited Jesus Christ into his life. I'm glad I took a chance and "just walked down the street" to meet a new friend.

Chapter *Three*

Right Where You Are

Evangelism is more often a matter of perspective than it is place. We might imagine that there are places in the world where the harvest fields are more plentiful than our little corner garden. The fascinating stories of missionaries ignite our imagination and we wonder at the work of God in distant lands. We consider the Apostle Paul, the great evangelist to the Gentiles, and recall his travels and adventures in city after city. Evangelism as an adventure seems more suited to new places and cultures than it does our own back yard. The adventure, however, is in the perspective. When we begin to see the world we live in, the routine we follow, with an eternal perspective, it is as if a new world has been opened to us . . . right where we are.

The ordinary landscape of our lives becomes God's field, with so much to pay attention to. There are hardened hearts that need a careful turning over, to encourage an openness to the things of God. There are seeds of truth that need to be planted and left to germinate in the minds and hearts of those that receive them. There are opportunities to quench the hunger and thirst of those seeking answers, hope, or help beyond their own ability or reach. There are people ready to be awakened to the brilliance and glory of the Son! There are those who need spiritual nurture that they might bloom and grow, bearing the beautiful Fruit of the Spirit.

Such a perspective invites us to an adventure with God. This perspective could overwhelm us unless we are wise to remember the words of the Apostle Paul in all of our field work.

"I planted the seed, Apollos watered it, but God made it grow. So neither he who plants nor he who waters is anything, but only God, who makes things grow. The one who plants and the one who waters have one purpose, and each will be rewarded according to their own labor. For we are God's fellow workers . . ." (1 Cor. 3: 6-9)

We are God's fellow workers! Isn't that perspective enough for a lifetime of adventure? Working with God, our faithfulness to the work set before us, God's faithfulness in bringing the growth. It is His work to save and to supply all that is needed for the task He invites us to.

In the stories that follow you will see how God worked to transform the perspective of His faithful ones to recognize the opportunities for evangelism in a thrift store and intake office. They testify to the adventure of working with God to say something . . . right where they are.

DODGE CITY, KANSAS

Historically known as a cattle town with a wild western history, Dodge City is in western Kansas, where the ground is hard, best suited as pasture, and where only prairie grass and tumble weeds seem likely to thrive.

Today, this community of approximately 30,000 continues to be influenced by the cattle industry. The ground is still hard and so is life. The small corps there had boasted no more than 25 in Sunday attendance for a decade or more, an indication of hard hearts and challenging spiritual soil. Appointed to this wild place were two faithful and hopeful servants of God. They saw in these dusty flint hills the potential for growth of something wonderful and new. Captains Joaquin and Gabriela Rangel arrived in Dodge City in July 2006. The Rangels ministered with passion and vision, praying for God to help them reach the lost and broken with the gospel.

There was little response to encourage them, but they would not be dissuaded from the work God had given them. Hearts were hard, but they believed that nothing is impossible for God. Five years of faithful and challenging preparation led them to reach up to God for answers and reach out to those around them for help. They needed a team to minister to this community effectively and began to prayerfully make plans to attend the National Seminar on Evangelism in 2011.

It was no coincidence that the executive representatives from the Central Territory that year were Majors Charles and Sharon Smith of the Kansas and Western Missouri Division. This was an answer to prayer. A letter was sent out to encourage participation in the seminar, to which the Dodge City Corps immediately responded. Captains Joaquin and Gabriela Rangel and five of their soldiers applied to be considered as delegates.

Once the members of the team were identified and invited to prepare their hearts and minds for this opportunity, the conversation turned to how to pay the registration costs. The team organized tamale sales and special fund-raising efforts to cover their registration and travel; however, the amount raised was not sufficient. When the division heard about the great effort the corps had made to raise funds, the decision was made to provide the remaining balance from a divisional evangelism fund. However, the division added an accountability component to the grant.

The corps had a thrift store that lacked sufficient staffing to stay open six days a week. The corps officers had been working in the store every Saturday to support the corps and to provide a needed ministry for the community. The division required the soldiers to volunteer in the thrift store for a minimum of six Saturdays. It was intended that they use that time to implement the training they would receive at NSE through the *Walk Across the Room* curriculum. The officers and soldiers were thrilled with the offer and accepted the challenge.

Expectations were high as this team arrived at Glen Eyrie for training. They were confident in the training they would receive and expectant of confirmation and direction from God. As is so often true when it comes to God's gifts to us, He had so much more in store for them. Truly they learned new skills, were given evangelistic tools, and were provided with a perspective and practice that would prove most encouraging. How delighted they were to also find that God met them early in the morning as they hiked the trails and took in the natural wonder and listened for God's voice in creation. They were drawn closer to God and one another as the morning worship and Bible studies led them to the top of one spiritual mountain after another.

Small groups played a pivotal role in the transformation of hearts and minds. They worked through personal challenges together and thrilled to the new heights to which God had brought them. The week on this Mountain of God had awakened them to the generosity of God for His people. One might expect that this group would despair at having to leave this beautiful and holy place; however, the Dodge City team would return to the valley with renewed faith. They would return to the hard soil of trampled lives and flint-like hearts with a zeal and joy to share what they had seen and heard on the Mountain of God.

The excitement would build as they returned home to western Kansas. Though it was no mountaintop, the perspective they had gained in the heights somehow transformed that ordinary place. The thrift store was so much more than a place to offer gently used items at fair prices. It was more than financial support to the ongoing work of The Salvation Army in that community. The store was now a field of opportunity; intentional engagement would lead to conversation, perhaps even friendship. Opportunities abounded for the sharing of the gospel in both proclamation and demonstration. This team returned to the dusty valley that had now become a field ripe for harvest.

Using the tools and skills gained at the seminar and following through on the promised volunteer hours, this team was able to form relationships with patrons of the store. In just one year's time three women joined Women's Ministries and others have shown interest in corps programs. One patron offered to assist the corps with their sound system on Sundays and provided his own equipment for an evangelistic outreach event.

On the day of the event the unit leaders, Majors Charles and Sharon Smith were present to witness the soldiers who had participated in the training and taken on leadership roles. About 60 to 70 people were in attendance. Full families gathered to hear the gospel proclaimed, share a meal and enjoy games and activities together. When the invitation was given to accept Christ as Savior and to live for Him, of the six people standing, two could be specifically identified as thrift store contacts.

When one of the new seekers was asked if she owned a Bible and indicated she did not, the trained soldier was seen removing her personal items from a newly purchased Bible and offering it to this new Christ-follower. The demonstration of the gospel matched the proclamation in generosity and genuine love.

Right where they were, this faithful and trusting group of believers offered themselves to the transforming work of God in their own lives and to His mission in Dodge City, Kansas. In His faithfulness He has not disappointed them. The dusty cattle town continues to be a field of great harvest as these faithful ones speak to the wonders they have experienced in the power and presence of God.

THE OTHER SIDE OF THE DESK

Major Kyle Trimmer knew Shona Heineman as a shy child. When he was appointed to Prescott, Arizona, as her corps officer, he found the same quiet Shona teaching in a preschool. But he and his wife recognized a characteristic they needed in another area of corps ministry and put her to work as the social service director at the Prescott, Arizona, Corps. Shona has an incredible capacity to love people, a trait the Trimmers saw as crucial to the ministry of this Salvation Army office. They had the vision to see that the people who would come through the door of this office had needs that might not be visible, but were very real.

The Major recalls the days with Shona at NSE. This seminar would be a challenge for Shona, and Major Trimmer was concerned that even connecting with other delegates could prove difficult. While at the seminar he took note of a change in his social service director. Not only was she making connections, but he often discovered her leading the discussions. He was thrilled to watch as Shona moved out on her own on the practice day, to speak with people and share the love of Jesus.

Shona Heineman has had many opportunities to share God's love with a variety of people on a daily basis. She has done this primarily through a demonstration of the gospel. Her comfort zone in Salvation Army mission is "meeting human need in His name without discrimination." Behind the desk there is a sense of professional security as she interviews people and gains insight into the issues they face. But after attending the National Seminar on Evangelism, Shona gained confidence and courage to step out from behind her desk to intentionally discuss matters of faith and to provide the spiritual support that is needed in times of crisis. "I am generally shy when it comes to talking to people about my faith," she says, "but the training at NSE opened my eyes to the broader picture of serving God in ways I never thought possible."

Once the interview concludes, the physical action of stepping around the desk signals that Shona, the professional, has now become Shona, the person. Both her vulnerability and genuine interest are evident as she goes beyond her clients' immediate physical needs to target their spiritual needs.

Shona finds herself in an incredible field of opportunity and God has helped her to recognize the ministry available to her beyond the interview. People come to The Salvation Army in need. They face challenges and difficulties and come looking for someone to help and guide them. They may come for help with a financial burden or guidance in finding housing or food. Because Shona Heineman loves and trusts Jesus, they may return home with more than they could have imagined—more hope, more courage, more grace, more power—and a friend in the faith. Here is one story she shares.

"A woman and her adult daughter came into our office seeking assistance with an electric bill. As I gathered information the question arose as to why they were unable to pay the bill. As we began to talk she shared with me that her husband was in the final stages of terminal cancer and that he would be admitted into hospice care the next day. We continued through the details of her financial need. I then took the opportunity to inquire about her emotional and spiritual needs. I invited her family to attend our corps programs. I gave her details regarding the youth ministries that were available to her younger children who would soon be dealing with the death of their dad. Before she left I walked around the desk and asked her if I might pray with her. She tearfully accepted. So we huddled together praying, all of us in tears. What a blessing it was to be able to bring comfort to someone going through such a difficult situation!"

Experiences like this one have given Shona the encouragement she needed to continue to share her faith and offer a word of prayer right where she is. Since her attendance at the seminar she has invited many people to corps programs. Several have attended, including a number who joined the corps Bible study. The number of children attending the youth programs has increased as well. In addition, Shona has begun to share a daily devotional with those who come to the Army's soup kitchen. She feels encouraged by those who have thanked her for that ministry.

Shona speaks to a transformation of perspective. "There are many more stories of people that I have had the opportunity to pray with, and lives that God has touched through me, all of which I would not have been as comfortable doing if it were not for my attendance at NSE."

"Shona is building an incredible bridge from our social service ministries to our corps," says Major Trimmer. The bridge Shona has built began with a decision to move out of her comfort zone and step around the desk. God hasn't changed her personality, but He has given her courage to move as He has directed to do what He designed her to do . . . to love people into His kingdom. Shona is saying something right where God has placed her.

Imagine the adventure open to us in The Salvation Army. There are many thrift stores, intake offices, gymnasiums, soup kitchens, craft rooms, parking lots, prayer rooms and a host of other fields we might be invited to work in. These aren't places we jump into without thought or purpose. We must prayerfully and carefully work with God to intentionally bring forth a harvest of lives transformed with new and eternal purpose. But we can do it. We can speak to the wonder and power of God in our lives. We can testify to His grace and mercy. We can speak of the change He has made and is making in our hearts and minds. We can say something . . . right where we are.

Chapter *Four*

Growing In Grace

Precious is the gift of salvation that we have received. Each one who has experienced the freedom and grace provided by Jesus Christ has a testimony to the wonder and power of it. God comes to us with the same offer of reconciliation and fullness of life, but He comes to each person in a way that is unique to that individual. Every story is different, as different as the person who owns it. As witnesses, these stories are to be shared—both God's story of redemptive love and the story of how that love has changed our lives. This can sometimes be difficult to define. One of the great blessings provided by the National Seminar on Evangelism is to reflect again on the wonder of salvation, to consider God's work in our lives and to put that work to words. This can be a life changing experience for a delegate. The power of the story first touches the heart of the one who owns it and then, when shared with renewed clarity and passion, has an impact on those with whom they live and work and play.

Many are the testimonies of the influence and impact of the National Seminar on Evangelism. The Glen is a sanctified space, inviting delegates to come away from the distractions of busy, noisy lives that they might hear the whisper of God. Their hearts are tuned to His voice through daily worship and Bible studies. They are reminded of His lavish love and generosity as they consider the gospel message and its impact on their own lives. They are invited to worship in the wonder and grandeur of this natural cathedral.

Those who have come expecting to meet God and to grow in grace have returned home changed. The change in the individual is difficult to measure or define, but it affects those with whom they come in contact in precious and powerful ways. The impact of attendance at this seminar has impacted the saints in this chapter. Their lives have embraced countless people with the love of Jesus. They testify about the meaningful milestone that this seminar had marked in their own journey with God.

THE LAME SHALL WALK

By Colonel Rodolph Lanier

Colonel Emily Lanier had not been able to walk without crutches for at least 10 years. To negotiate the 46 steps at the entrance to Glen Eyrie, she had to be carried in a chair. She had endured eight surgeries to alleviate a herniated disc, and the scar tissue left her in as much pain as her original spinal problems. In 1979 a prayer team was formed at the NSE, which included Captain Robert Johnson, Major Damon Rader and delegates Hubert Phillips and Chuck Wright. These four men, who had never met before, came from each of the four territories in The Salvation Army. They discussed their backgrounds, Christian experience and the purpose and power of prayer in Christian living and evangelizing. And they began to pray.

After a few prayer sessions, the group began to feel led to pray for healing, specifically for Colonel Lanier, even though they did not know the details of her debilitating condition. But first they needed a sign. The next morning Captain Johnson met her at breakfast in the dining room, and they spent time getting acquainted before the first NSE session began. Clearly sensing the presence of the Holy Spirit, he knew that he was "standing on holy ground." Without a doubt this was the confirmation the team had been seeking.

That evening the prayer team, joined by Dr. Roger Green and Captain George Price, met in a lounge adjacent to Emily's room to discuss Scriptural accounts of healing as well as their own stories of personal soul-searching. Although surprised and a little bewildered, when Emily was told that God's promises would be claimed, she agreed to join the group. Together they prayed boldly and fervently that she would be healed and empowered to resume the ministry that was God's plan for her life. Obeying the scriptural imperative in James 5:14-15, they also anointed her with oil.

Then each man prayed aloud, and one of them told her to stand up and walk. "Hand me my crutch," she responded as usual. "Stand up and walk, you won't be needing the crutches again," he said. And she did, first tenuously and then with confidence! On August 23, 1979, at 1:30 p.m., this group witnessed a joyous moment of affirmation that the kingdom is right here, that Jesus wants us to be whole, and that miracles occur today just as they did in the first century.

Emily's prayer was one of total submission to the will of God. There were no ifs, ands or buts attached. She knew that whatever happened, she was yoked to Christ and safe in the kingdom. "Lord, I want what you want for me! If You want me dead; If You want me alive; If you want me sick; If you want me well; THAT'S WHAT I WANT!" The next morning, her muscles and limbs fully functioning, her pain permanently gone, she climbed the steps to breakfast unaided. A few months later she wrote to her father and stepmother, Majors E.V. and Jewell Farmer, "I have suddenly become very active overnight. We have been away every weekend. I get very tired, as you can imagine. The rest of me is not quite up to my legs yet, but what a wonderful experience!" It was a mighty demonstration of spiritual power that glorified the Trinity and gave Emily another 12 years of active service in The Salvation Army, a total of 43 years as an officer.

MAJOR TIMOTHY THOMAS

By Katherine Adams

On December 31, 1959, midnight was approaching. Lt. Colonel Lyell Rader was preaching as Timothy L. Thomas came to pick up his five children from The Salvation Army. When he arrived, they were all kneeling at the altar. He could not understand why they were asking God to forgive them. They were children, and in his mind they hadn't done anything wrong. He, on the other hand had much to repent for. Timothy joined his children at the altar and as he reached up, God reached down and touched his life in such a profound way that he testified to an experience similar to that of Paul on the road to Damascus. The encounter with God was transformative.

Timothy Thomas was Promoted to Glory in 2004 but until the day he died, he couldn't stop telling people about what happened on New Year's Eve of 1959. His children will tell you that he never passed up an opportunity to proclaim the love the Lord had put in his hardened heart.

Katherine Adams was there the night her dad was saved. She was only seven years old, but she knew that when she woke up the next morning her father was a different person. She recalls that her dad immediately stopped smoking two packs a day, drinking liquor and whatever else grownups did outside of God's will. Katherine remembers sitting in the back seat of the family car asking her brothers, "Does Dad have to tell everybody about Jesus?" as their father pumped gas at the service station.

Major Grace Thomas, Tim's wife, says that he was selected along with a handful of others in the Western Pennsylvania division to attend The National Soldier's Seminar on Evangelism. Tim was a soldier in The Salvation Army who had been recommended by the Homewood corps officer, Captain William Buzzard. He and the other delegates drove to Colorado Springs to attend the seminar. What a road trip it turned out to be for all of them! Participation in the seminar unveiled spiritual strategies for witnessing and winning others to God. The group prayed to overcome their shortcomings and to learn all they could about evangelizing. Tim and his new colleagues in Christ fasted and prayed every Thursday for years, and God increased in them all.

Many souls were introduced to the Lord and many more were saved. Tim became a corps sergeant major, completed his GED and heeded God's call to the ministry. Grace made the commitment, too, and together they entered The Salvation Army's School for Officer's Training. Later, Tim would serve on the staff at this seminar. God's road trip took them to New York, Springfield, Hartford, Boston, Harlem and many other places to preach the Word and the love of Jesus. Glen Eyrie was one of the first stops on a road trip with God that lasted 25 years in The Salvation Army.

MAJOR DARLENE HARVEY

My history with the NSE started in the 1980s and continues to this day. When I was a teenager, some of the leaders in my corps attended NSE and returned with glowing testimonies. In 1986, my husband and I were privileged to attend NSE as soldiers. I remember loading the bus at the airport and driving to Glen Eyrie in Colorado Springs. The beauty of the majestic mountains and all of God's creation ignited our expectation that something extraordinary would happen during that week. We were indeed on holy ground.

Before attending NSE, I had a strong desire to share Christ with others, but I was uncertain about how to proceed. The person who was heavy on my heart was my dad. When I returned home, the Holy Spirit gave me an opportunity to talk to him. I shared what I had learned and led him to the Lord. It is a moment that has made me forever grateful.

After I became a corps officer, my husband and I saw NSE as a great opportunity to train soldiers in evangelism as well as to broaden their experience of The Salvation Army. As a corps officer, I have accompanied soldiers in 1994, 1999, 2009 and 2010. It has been exciting to see them grow in their passion to share Christ's love, especially in practical ways. I have seen evangelism training evolve from a specific, memorized plan into a more natural way of sharing God's action in our lives. I have also seen God use many different methods of evangelism when there is a loving sensitivity to the Holy Spirit's promptings.

God has used NSE to inspire me as an officer and to renew my commitment to the priority of evangelism. He brought good out of evil after my family endured a terrible crisis. One Monday in October 1998, my husband, Dave, and I were preparing to go to officers' councils. When I came home from the store, Dave's car was in the driveway, and I knew something was wrong. He came out to meet me and in a broken voice, told me that my dad had been murdered. In shock, I felt like I watched events unfold from somewhere above. It was as if I were in a dream—a nightmare, really.

I prayed that we would know what had happened to my dad. My brothers had been trying to contact him since Friday. We had no idea how long he'd been dead.

Even through this tragedy we saw God working. On his way to the morgue on Tuesday, my brother spotted my dad's stolen car in Detroit. This led to the arrest of the person who'd killed my father. By the time my dad was buried later that week, we had a full confession through a lie detector test and knew many of the details. God had answered my prayers by revealing the circumstances behind his death.

Incredibly, the person who killed my dad was the brother of my best friend from childhood. When I was eight, this friend had brought me to Sunbeams and introduced me to The Salvation Army.

Following my mother's death in 1986, my father became a Christian and occasionally went to The Salvation Army. There he met and married my friend's mother, though the marriage lasted only a year. Unknown to us, after their divorce her son had visited my dad periodically to ask for money for drugs. On one of those evenings, he became angry. He not only took my dad's money and car but took his life.

A very difficult year followed for me. I felt personally responsible for Dad's death, which was violent and tragic. If it had not been for my involvement with the Army, I thought, maybe he wouldn't have met the person who killed him. Often our Army clients reminded me of the man who'd killed my dad. I wanted to start a new chapter in my life, and for the first—and only—time I thought about resigning as an officer. But God always knows what we need and makes it available when we need it.

That summer at a women's camp meeting a guest sang about heaven, and I bawled uncontrollably. Afterward the speaker could see that something was terribly wrong. I told her about my dad, and, though neither of us could believe it, her dad also had been murdered that same year. The book *What's So Amazing about Grace*, by Philip Yancey, had really helped her. I soon found myself reading it, and it aided my own process of healing.

During the summer of 1999, I participated in the NSE for the third time. My college roommate prayed with me on the patio of the castle, asking God to replace my memory of Dad's murder with loving and positive memories. God reminded me that though my dad had lost his earthly life, he had found salvation—and I had played a part in that decision.

God also used that summer to show me the self-righteousness in my own life and my need to extend grace. I returned home from NSE renewed in my passion to be an officer and more strongly committed to sharing Christ with others. I think I had been self-righteous about the decisions I'd made, taking credit for the good things in my life rather than praising them as gifts and grace from God. Without even realizing it, I'd developed a judgmental attitude toward people who had addictions. I thought they'd made bad choices and would have to live with the consequences. I did not have Christ's compassion.

Although I'd long ago memorized Ephesians 2:8-9, these verses became more real to me: "For it is by grace you have been saved, through faith—and this not from yourselves, it is the gift of God." Often we are reluctant to receive or extend God's grace, and often our problems are rooted in this reticence. We either cannot forgive ourselves or accept forgiveness, or we do not forgive others and hang onto bitterness.

While we were stationed in Green Bay, Wisconsin, I had an opportunity to attend a program at the local prison on restorative justice taught by one of our corps members. It gave me a different perspective, more understanding and compassion for people who have committed crimes. I thank God I have forgiven the person who killed my dad. I know I did not do this in my own strength but God's, as we read in Philippians 4:13.

My dad's life reminds me of the Easter story. He was a loving man who did not deserve to die a violent death. While he lay dying, what few possessions he had were discarded and sold. He was alone for three days before he was found. Just as Jesus conquered death and rose again giving us victory, I know that God has given me victory through gratitude for my own salvation and the opportunity to share my experience with others. This is the story—the gospel story and our personal story—we are taught to share at NSE.

Since 1999, I have had the opportunity to go to Glen Eyrie three more times. I took soldiers there from the Chicago Kroc Center in 2009 and 2010. God also granted me a desire of my heart when I was asked to serve on staff at NSE in 2010 and 2011. It has been wonderful to see people grow in their relationship with the Lord through NSE. People come with different levels of experience in sharing the gospel and leave with more passion and tools for sharing their story. It is also beautiful to see how friendships that last a lifetime have been formed during this week long seminar. People see the large family in The Salvation Army that reaches across the nation and around the world, and we learn how to enlarge God's family by leading others to Christ.

Additionally, it is wonderful to see God's grace evoked through soldiers and officers who have come with their own hurts, as I did in 1999. God has healed their hearts and renewed their covenant with their first love. When a delegate comes to NSE, he or she returns home a different person. This transformation leads to changed lives and an expansion of God's kingdom.

Obviously, the National Seminar on Evangelism isn't the only sacred place God uses to come close to His saints and fan into flame the passion and purpose of their lives, to love God with all their being and love their neighbor perfectly. Still, it has for years provided Salvationists with the opportunity to come away to a quiet place, perhaps for the first time, for the purpose of refocusing their thoughts, words and actions on the work of evangelism. Here they have been encouraged to reflect on the work of God in their lives and put that story into words that would clearly and carefully convey the most wonderful story of love—God's story.

The seminar invites delegates to come and grow in grace. The result of the cessation of work and concentration on the Word, and the opportunity to practice, immediately, the skills they have learned makes a difference in the life of the attendee. Whether they hone skills in the ability to initiate conversation, to direct a friend to spiritual matters or to clearly testify to God's power at work within them, these saints have met with God and cannot keep it to themselves. They must share. They must *say something*. God's work at Glen Eyrie is transformed into God's words to a broken and needy world. A world these good people have been encouraged to embrace with Spirit-breathed words of love.

Chapter *Five*

You Never Know

My family enjoys hiking in the mountains. Each year we have made our pilgrimage to Rocky Mountain National Park for restoration and recreation of body, mind and spirit. On our hikes we see glorious sights and take in the lessons that live in the flowers and streams and peaks. We often meet people on the trail. If our pace allows we may engage in conversation or pause to hear a bit about the journey and adventure of those we meet. That is where we met Joe. Joe is a retired Methodist preacher. He was nearing his 80th birthday and was out on the trail to celebrate.

Joe had spent many of his summers in the mountains on the trails. When he learned of our work and ministry with The Salvation Army, he was eager to share of his experience and love for the Army and we slowed our pace. Stories were shared about ministry and opportunity. We paused at the place where our paths parted to delight in the fellowship and companionship God had provided. Joe took a breath and a light went on in his eyes.

"I love to hike up here because you just never know who you are going to meet, or what might come of the conversation," he said. "It's hard to tell where people are coming from or where they are headed. God knows, though, and I'm glad for the company He sends my way. I like to make the first move in conversation . . . ask a question or two, maybe share a story about the trail or area they are hiking to. But then I do a fair bit of listening . . . to them, to God. As I step off on the trail I ask the Lord to make me a blessing. I don't always get confirmation on that, but I am ready to lead where He follows." With a quick wink he was off, and soon engaged in conversation with others as they moved near him on the trail.

I wondered at Joe's words. I would soon be traveling to Glen Eyrie to greet the delegates of NSE. I thought about Joe's familiarity on the trail and the easy way he engaged us as we moved closer together. I thought about the opportunities God had given Joe for ministry as a Methodist preacher and as a hiker. I pondered the light in Joe's eyes when he said, "You never know . . ." Joe was ready for engagement, and expectant, but completely delighted by God's wonderful and mysterious ways. How can we know what He has in mind? It is impossible, but we can be ready and expectant, delighting in those He brings near us as we travel on the path He has directed us to follow.

SEEKING A PERSONAL GOD

Thursday of the National Seminar on Evangelism is a day looked upon with great anticipation and anxiety. This is the day that all of the training has led up to, the day the delegates have had in mind since arriving on the grounds. Thursday is "E" Day, Evangelism Day! After the delegates worship together in music and Bible study they collect a bag lunch and load the buses. The buses are quiet on their journey to parks and malls and Salvation Army service centers. Delegates pray and diligently try to recall all that has been shared over the past few days of study and preparation. The spirit in those buses is often very different on the return trip, and the banter spills out and fills the Castle terrace where both joy and relief is tangible. God is always faithful to delight and surprise the delegates, and their stories are shared with praise to the Lord for His kindness and encouragement.

Gina Forlenza was with a group that visited a park. A band was playing in the park and people had gathered to listen. Gina and her partner sat down in the grass with a young couple. While her partner engaged the young woman in conversation, Gina attempted to speak with the young man over the loud sounds of the band. Conversation was challenging, but Gina felt compelled to make a connection. She discovered that the young man had recently experienced the death of his brother. The separation was difficult and he wore his brother's hat with a great deal of sentimentality. Gina asked her new friend if he believed in God. "Oh, I believe that there is a being who created the world," he told her, "but I don't believe in a personal God."

They continued in conversation about his brother and the funeral. The young man's mother had not attended the event and he hadn't spoken to her in some time. The band that had been playing so loudly paused for a moment. Gina could sense the sorrow and tension as he shared this part of his story and asked if she could pray with him. He accepted her offer. She asked God to help this man and his mother mend their relationship and to bring peace and comfort in this time of grief. After the "amen" his phone rang. He glanced at the number listed and a look of astonishment appeared on his face. "It's my mom!" he told Gina. The band started up again and the young man took the call. The bus had arrived to take Gina back to the Glen, signaling the end to this encounter. She had seen the look of wonder in the face, and heard the sound of happiness in the voice of the young man in the park.

Does the young man believe in God? Gina doesn't know. But she was thrilled to have been there and watched as God made Himself known to the young man in the park. Her obedience to speak, over the sounds of the band, opened a window in the soul of a stranger. The light and breath of God came through. At the same time it encouraged the faith and commitment of Gina Forlenza. You never know what God has in mind. But we can be sure that it will always be exceedingly, abundantly more than all we can ask or imagine.

Major Sheryl Tollerud is no stranger to evangelism. She has been trained in several evangelistic systems and been given a number of tools. At a young age she recalls memorizing scripts that would be used during Vacation Bible School to invite people to attend the weekly classes and activities. She participated in the Salvation Army tradition of open air meetings, which were held on street corners and in parks with opportunities for soldiers to give a testimony, sing a hymn and preach the word to passers by. She attended a Billy Graham crusade at age 14, where she committed her life to Christ. Sheryl attended a number of corps evangelistic seminars that provided training in use of "The Four Spiritual Laws," "Spirit-Filled Life" and "Evangelism Explosion."

She was privileged to attend the National Soldiers' Seminar on Evangelism and to witness the miracle of healing in Colonel Emily Lanier's life. She attended CFOT courses on evangelism training, understanding and accepting the responsibility of every believer to be a witness for Jesus. Even with all of that experience and training she still felt very uncomfortable with what she called "cold turkey" witnessing, and struggled in the practice of such evangelism. As a divisional leader, Sheryl was offered the opportunity to attend the seminar again as a unit leader, but this time with Bill Hybel's "Walk Across the Room" curriculum.

She was delighted with what she heard and learned during the week and a hunger had grown in her heart for opportunities to put it all into practice. This made sense to her—Develop Friendship, Discover Stories, Discern Next Steps—all empowered and directed by the Holy Spirit. She loved the freedom this material provided and the weight of responsibility felt so much different. During the covenant service she recognized for the first time that she possessed the gift of evangelism! It was both a discovery and a joy as the realization came over her. She loves to teach this material because, she says, "It is for EVERYONE!"

Major Tollerud has had a number of opportunities to exercise this gift in her life and ministry. Here is one story she shares with us.

SIRI

Shortly after attending the NSE in Denver last summer, I was privileged to travel to Greece and Turkey on a study tour. The flight to our first destination would take more than 11 hours, and my husband and I had reserved window and aisle seats. Our custom was that if the third passenger were a man, my husband would move to the middle, and if a woman arrived to join us, I would take the center seat. My husband would usually laugh and say, "the fervent prayer of a righteous man availeth much," if a woman came. On this laborious trip, he was delighted to see a woman unloading her carry on bag into the overhead compartment. I offered her the aisle seat, which meant my husband could lean against the window and sleep for hours, leaving me stuck in the middle!

While making polite conversation, I asked the woman about her travel plans. Siri was returning to Iran to visit her daughter, but she was very upset because she had just left her mother, who was dying and only expected to live a few more days. I asked her why she had chosen to travel now, and she replied that this was the only time her son-in-law would allow her to visit her daughter and grandchildren. Her mother had told her, "I love you very much. Good-bye. Now go visit the living!"

Siri had fled Iran during an era of persecution and was very unhappy when her son-in-law decided to move the family back to their native country. She was visibly shaken and sad. I tried to share some words of comfort and to get to know her. After the plane took off I asked Siri if her faith was helping her during this difficult time. She smiled at me and replied, "I am Muslim, not a Christian." I said I thought so because of her nationality, but I was still interested in whether or not her faith helped her to cope with stressful circumstances. Siri immediately replied, "No, of course, no."

It was a sad answer, so I quickly said a prayer and then gently added, "Well, during times like this my faith is what I rely on." I told her that my father had died a couple of years earlier, and my mother was not well. Every time I visited my mother, I knew it could be the last time, so I empathized with the difficulty of having to say good-bye. I shared that as a Christian, my God supports me with His strength and grace during times of crisis. I added that she might know that as a Christian I believed that Jesus, God's Son, came to earth to become my Savior, dying on the cross. "Because He rose from the dead, I know I will see my parents again in heaven. They are the ones who taught me faith in Jesus Christ," I said. We sat in silence for a long time, both of us resting and me praying.

After awhile I said that I had been praying for her, her mother and her daughter. I could only imagine how torn she felt. Siri thanked me. Then I felt prompted to ask about the situation she would encounter in Iran. Would she be under her son-in-law's authority or allowed to travel freely? She said she would be under his authority and that being back in Iran would be challenging. She was a bit scared and unsure of what lay ahead, but she desperately wanted to see her daughter and grandchildren again. The conversation led to family life and other topics, and then we rested again.

When the plane landed we exchanged best wishes for each other's visits. As Siri walked down the aisle to deboard she suddenly stopped, turned around and came back to give me a hug, saying, "Thank you for your prayers." I don't really know what all Siri understood, but since that time

I have kept her name in my Bible and do pray for her regularly. Maybe someone else will continue to share the story of Christ with her and lead her to salvation.

Major Tollerud couldn't have imagined what God had in mind on that trip. We can wonder with her at God's mysterious ways. He reveals Himself to those He loves and invites us to participate in that revelation. Our willingness to move to the middle seat, so to speak, may not only make a difference in the life of the one beside us, but it has an effect on us as well. We listen carefully to His whispered words and wait for that nudge to share that truth and whispered love with the one He places on the journey next to us. It was evident in Siri's response as she left the plane that those words of grace and love had reached the one God desired to embrace.

MAJOR BRIAN GILLIAM

Major Brian Gilliam has been on staff at NSE for years and is one of the friendliest people you will ever meet. He has a smile and a story ready to share for every occasion. He possesses the gift of laughter and a listening ear. Major Gilliam is a people magnet and he is amazed at the number of people God has brought along his path to influence and love into the kingdom. "It is as if I am wearing a 'Talk to Me' sign that only others can see," he says. While he is standing in the checkout line at the grocer, enjoying a meal out or just walking through the mall, people approach him and tell them their problems and stories, often in intimate detail. The major could be bothered by this, but instead has chosen to make himself available . . . to God and to those who happen to read that invisible sign.

Here is what he has to say about those experiences.

"Of course, when these opportunities arise, I use good judgment in listening and then guide them so that our conversation moves toward Jesus and what He has done in my life. The thought has entered my mind, 'Really God? I just wanted to get a few groceries,' but then I am reminded of just how He works through us as we make ourselves open and available.

"Just the other day, a guy ran across the parking lot and retrieved my grocery cart just to have the opportunity to talk with me and share a burden on his heart. Wow! I am thankful I was ready and willing to spend the necessary time."

It makes you wonder what it is about the major that causes people to open up and share. Certainly the Holy Spirit is at work in all of this, preparing Brian's heart and mind and spirit as well as preparing those who are traveling along beside him. Awareness and openness to the opportunities around us are important tools God uses in evangelism, as is the careful preparation of heart, mind and spirit.

In a recent testimony, staff member Patricia Kukuc described her NSE experience:

"Attending the seminar, both as a delegate and as support staff, made me realize that if I'm going to witness to others, then my life must reflect Jesus all the time. I want people to know by my actions and by my conversation that I belong to Jesus Christ. That means committing daily to studying God's Word and listening to Him, so that I really know Him."

Pat's words are challenging. Jesus told a story about 10 virgins who were invited to a wedding. Some had lamps with plenty of oil, while others had to leave to replenish their supply. While the latter were away, the bridegroom arrived and those with oil in their lamps were invited to the party. We often use that story to illustrate God's invitation to salvation through Jesus Christ. But what about all of these opportunities to join God in His amazing work of redeeming and restoring lives? I wonder how many "parties" I have missed when the bridegroom arrived and I was running on empty. How many opportunities have been met with annoyance rather than availability? I am challenged to reflect Jesus, to lift Him up and say something about what He has done in my life, and that He will "draw all people to (Himself)" (John 12:32).

SOWING SEEDS IN THE HEARTLAND

By Lt. Colonel Nita Lodge

When Ed Walton was sent to the NSE, he was already an active Salvationist. But the experience at Glen Eyrie so inspired him that when he returned home he wanted to do something more to reach the neighborhoods around him and his corps. Noticing unused copies of the *War Cry*, he struck upon an idea and began a ministry that has blessed countless homes in the St. Louis area.

"Lord, move on my spirit to use this tool for You," he prayed. Having read many issues, he was convinced that the articles were intended for blessing people, encouraging them and introducing them to the Savior. He sensed that God had commissioned him as a seed-sower, a kind of Salvationist Johnny Appleseed, through distribution of the *War Cry*.

He began greeting neighbors with, "On behalf of the Good Lord above, and His Son Jesus, our Savior, we wish you a blessed day," and offering them a copy of the *War Cry*.

To further personalize each issue of the *War Cry*, Ed designs a label with appropriate graphics and Scripture to apply to the cover. Careful to respect the wishes of his neighbors, he honors all "no solicitors" signs. It's not uncommon for people to offer money, but Ed makes every effort to let them know that he isn't trying to collect funds. He returns to the corps any money people insist on giving, and donates any gifts–in–kind to the nearest Adult Rehabilitation Center.

When promoting the *War Cry* he often describes the features as stories to help with the rough times in life. Many times this has led to personal conversation, often resulting in prayer. He has had many pivotal and transforming encounters over three years and 180–200 *War Cry* deliveries.

For instance, while visiting a garage sale, one family told him that their teenage daughter had turned her life around through a Salvation Army rehabilitation program that helps young people find direction. Thanks to the compassionate tough love of the counselors, the young woman was reunited with her grateful family.

Ed noticed a For Sale sign in front of a house in his neighborhood. The owner shared that he had lost his job and had to sell the house and move away. Ed prayed with the man about the sale of his home and for comfort for his family during the difficult transition.

Ed testifies to God's year-round provision for daily strength and receptive hearts. His only motive is to bring glory to God and to promote the Kingdom. God is honoring the efforts of this faithful servant. Ed's hope is that readers will be encouraged by his experiences and will prayerfully consider how they can be used to reach others for the Lord.

The truth is you never know who God may send your way. You can't predict His timing or His ways. You may never know the results. But readiness to share in spirit and in truth is all God needs to move someone toward faith. You never know who may come along as you travel your path, or what the conversation may lead to. But you can know that God is faithful, His ways are perfect and He loves to share in the joy of this work by inviting us to participate. I hope I am still hiking at age 80 and that I will welcome those along the way with enthusiasm and anticipation. I want to live prepared to participate with God and completely delighted in His wondrous and mysterious ways. I want to be like Joe, who most certainly hikes with God.

Glen Eyrie Castle

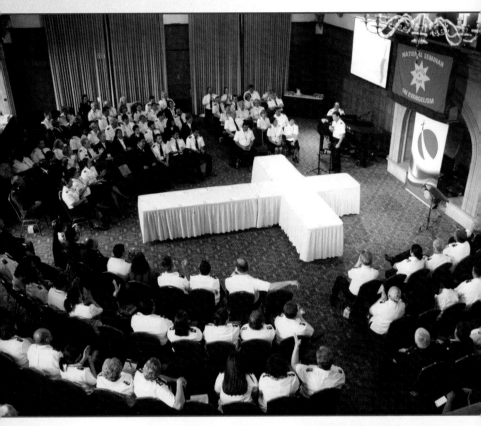

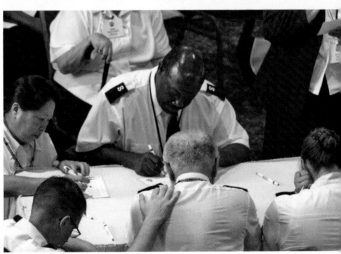

Covenant Service

Enjoying God's Good Creation

Worshipping Together and Blessing One Another

A Community of Faith

Conversation with God

"On the mountain of the Lord the Lord will provide."

Gen. 22:14

The Face of Christ

*"For wherever two
or three are gathered
in My name,
I am there..."*

Matt. 18:26

"My Word will not return to me empty."

Isaiah 55:11

1968 - Inaugural National Soldier's Seminar on Evangelism

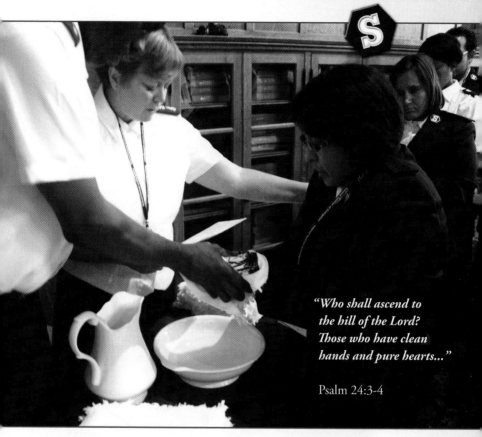

> *"Who shall ascend to the hill of the Lord? Those who have clean hands and pure hearts..."*
>
> Psalm 24:3-4

"My kingdom is not of this world."   John 18:36

TELL THEM. WIN THEM. ESTABLISH THEM.

*"The grass withers and the flowers fall, but
the word of our God endures forever."*

Isaiah 40:8

Chapter *Six*

When You Think
You've Failed

F aithfulness and obedience to the Holy Spirit may not always produce the results we hope for. The Spirit may say, "Go!" but the one we speak to may respond with "No." Perhaps our enthusiasm will be met with anger or violence. The opportunities may have presented themselves and we may have been frozen in fear, or stand unprepared to give a reason for the hope that is in us. We may ask God to make us a blessing to someone today and find ourselves having said nothing intentionally with those around us about the Lord of love and His gift of salvation. Whatever the failure, it can feel devastating.

RIDICULE AND REJECTION

Failure can provide an opportunity to deepen our dependence on God and trust His power to redeem all things. A negative response to the gospel isn't something that we should necessarily take as a sign that our words have not hit the mark God had intended. Perhaps we have been given the task of tilling some very hard ground. Truth can bring pain, and pain isn't often warmly welcomed. It is crucial to walk carefully with the Holy Spirit when dealing with hardened hearts and scarred lives. But we must be faithful to His leading and direction and trust the results to Him.

Jesus warned His disciples of certain rejection as He shared the Passover meal with them before His crucifixion and resurrection. In John's gospel we read His words,

"If the world hates you, keep in mind that it hated me first. If you belonged to the world, it would love you as its own. As it is, you do not belong to the world, but I have chosen you out of the world. That is why the world hates you . . . if they persecuted me, they will persecute you also." John 15:18-20

Jesus taught and healed and loved. He challenged the thinking of those He came in contact with and threatened their systems and the choices they made. His words and actions always hit their intended mark. Some people accepted Him, welcoming the transformation of their thinking, choices and lives. Others rejected Him violently. Jesus knew His disciples would face the same rejection and violence, so He encouraged them to remain in His love. With the knowledge of what must be accomplished for salvation to be available to all, Jesus demonstrated His love with His life and reminded His disciples that it is best to love, even if one is not loved in return. It is worth it!

Jesus' words continue to challenge and threaten us. Some will choose to welcome the change God wants to bring about in their lives. Others will reject Him, and in rejecting Him they reject us. But be reminded that to remain in His love is to be in a place of great blessing. It is still worth the risk to say something. Let the words hit their mark, and trust God to work in the hardest of hearts, in His way and in His time.

A LESSON IN REJECTION

Erin Jones applied for a teaching position at a school in East Aurora, Illinois. This school was situated in the heart of gang territory. Erin remembers feeling an evil presence as she entered the school for the first time; it was as if Satan had control of the place. The need of students and staff for the love of God was tangible. She found her way to her workspace, a room she shared with two other women. Upon entering the room she felt a wonderful radiant spirit of peace. After some time together, sharing personal stories and concerns, she discovered that these women were Christians. They shared a meaningful fellowship together as they prayed for one another and the students and staff in the school.

Many took notice of the difference in the lives of these women. It was reflected in the way they treated one another and in their responses to those around them. Students found more than a math specialist, reading specialist and intervention facilitator; they found the presence and spirit of Jesus. Though the women were denied the freedom to approach others on matters of faith, staff and students found their way to them with concerns and requests. Their room became a refuge for children with special needs and behavioral challenges. This was particularly true of students situated in a nearby classroom. The behavioral concerns in this room appeared to be escalating and worsening by the day. Violent outbursts and disrespect for the teacher and her assistant grew to a level needing intervention. Erin and her team were invited to help develop strategies for motivating students to learn and dealing with their challenging behaviors. They made this not only a professional goal, but determined to pray for this teacher and her students as well.

As the team sat down to work with the teacher, they began to offer suggestions, praying that the Holy Spirit would intercede and provide the needed solution to the issues at hand. "It was as if a switch was flipped," Erin recalls. "The teacher became defensive and her attitude turned hostile. She started to scream obscenities at us, accusing us of forcing our beliefs on her and the students. She then requested that we leave her room immediately." The women were stunned. They wondered about their words. Had they spoken of their faith in Christ, offered a prayer or freely testified to His power at work in them without notice? Was Jesus so much a part of their conversation and lives together that they had naturally spoken of Him? They could not recall. But there was no mistake that whatever was shared was used by God to touch this teacher, and the result was powerful rejection. The women continued to pray together, in no way inhibited in their faithful witness to this teacher and others in the school. Though the rejection had been painful and humiliating, they determined to answer it with love. It is what Jesus had called them to do, and they trusted His guidance and purpose.

Evangelism is about connecting people, made in God's image, with the One who made them and loves them best. These same people have been given the freedom to accept or reject His gift of salvation. Rejection could very well be a test of the love and grace we describe in our witness of Jesus Christ. It is important that we remain in His love at all times, but especially when that love is resisted. If we are genuinely concerned about those we speak to about salvation we will see them as more than tally marks or members. They will continue to be valued and loved as people who will one day no longer be able to resist the powerful grace of God.

While hiking in the mountains, I am never disappointed at the number and variety of wild flowers that bloom in some of the most rugged and challenging places along the trail. This fragile beauty has always intrigued me. These flowers bloom in places where they could very well go unnoticed and unappreciated. But they bloom all the same. It is what flowers do. In the same way, it is important not to let the hard and challenging opportunities keep us from saying something about Jesus and His power to forgive, cleanse, heal and transform lives. We must *say something* . . . it is what a witness does. So whether our words are welcomed or rejected, we must remember that it is best to love, even if one is not loved in return. It is worth it.

PURSUED BY THE ENEMY

A favorite literary character is Much Afraid, from Hannah Hurnard's book *Hind's Feet on High Places*. Much Afraid makes a journey with the Shepherd to the High Places. Though she faithfully follows the path the Shepherd has asked her to take, she continues to be pursued by her enemies. Pride and Fear follow her up the path, distracting and discouraging her. She is in no danger until she wanders out of reach of her traveling companion and into their waiting grasp. Her encounters with them bring humility and pain, but with the faintest cry for help they have no power to keep her from returning to the path and moving forward with her Shepherd close beside.

We can identify with Much Afraid. Pride and Fear are enemies we have all had dealings with, especially when it comes to the business of proclamation of the gospel. When we wander from the voice of our Shepherd we can fall victim to failure. It is often painful and humiliating, but it should not keep us from returning to the careful guidance of the Holy Spirit in our mission to share the love of Christ.

LINDA MATHIS

Linda Mathis is a small group leader who has served on the NSE staff. Linda has encouraged delegates to deepen their relationship with God and to trust His direction and leadership in the opportunities He provides. She has been an important cheerleader as delegates prepare for their practicum and day of engagement during the seminar. Tension is often great as the buses are loaded. There is a quiet contemplation and prayerful anticipation. When the buses return, the testimonies that fill the castle grounds are glowing and full of praise. Linda shares a story of a young man whose experience at the seminar was very different, but she has seen the evidence of transformation coming alive in this young man on the other side of failure.

"About three years ago delegates from my corps attended the NSE. Among them was a relatively new Christian named Chris. He had been attending the corps for a couple of years and had become a senior soldier. He faithfully wore his uniform and attended all the meetings he could. He believed that God had called him to Salvation Army officership. His desire to attend NSE stemmed from his desire to better prepare himself to fulfill his calling. He is a shy young man but very friendly when he gets to know someone. He is quick with a smile.

"He loved every minute he was there. He met many new people who quickly became his friends. Any apprehensions he had about the seminar faded. He absorbed everything and loved to discuss what he had learned with anyone who was willing. Because he was working on a degree in Christian Ministries, he would apply what he was learning at the seminar to what he was learning about the Bible through his college courses.

"Finally the day came for our outreach. His small group went to the mall. He was a little apprehensive but felt he was ready.

"When people were arriving back to the Glen Eyrie campus, I looked for Chris. I wanted to know how he did on the outreach. He hung his head and quietly said, 'I froze. I did not speak to anyone.' I put my arm around his shoulder and told him that the devil was working overtime today. He did not want any of us witnessing for the Lord. About that time Chris' small group instructor came over to us. He took Chris aside and talked to him.

"The next morning Chris was still a little down. He felt as though he had let God down. But God did not let go of Chris! I began to see a change in him at the corps. He became a bolder person, speaking out for God. He asked our corps officer for the opportunity to preach. When he did preach, he spoke with confidence, with boldness, with conviction. He began to teach the Adult Sunday School class, and on Wednesday nights, he began teaching our Bible study group.

"The devil intended to defeat Chris at NSE by playing on his fear of evangelism. But God reigned supreme! God turned that moment of defeat into a victory! The long term effects of that awful experience at the mall have been very positive in Chris's life. Chris learned that even in our lowest of lows, God is there. He promised never to leave us nor forsake us. He kept His promise to Chris."

Missed opportunities haunt us. Conversations come to mind when we sit quietly with the Lord and wonder how we could have missed the open door . . . with the neon sign staring us in the face saying, "Tell me about Jesus." We rehearse those scenes over and over in our minds imagining what might have happened if we had had the presence of mind to say something of eternal value instead of droning on about work or travel. We pray that God will make us a blessing to someone, but do we expect Him to do it? Those missed opportunities don't often repeat themselves. But missing them can cause us to grow more intentional in our thoughts and more deliberate in our words.

"SEND SOMEONE"

Major Darryl Leedom attended NSE in 1993, the year his daughter was born. He reflects on the time as inspiring and motivating in regard to his ministry to his first family. Being the only Christ follower in his family of origin he remembers making their salvation a matter of daily prayer and passionate petition before the Lord.

"My family was experiencing a great deal of turmoil. It seemed as though I was making regular trips to Nebraska for funerals, counseling or to offer support during health crises. Each visit was a poignant reminder of the difference God had made in my life. I had a source for dealing with all of these things that my brothers and sister, mom and dad, did not. It amazed me how readily my family members reached out to me during these times and how desperate they seemed to be for the strength God had given me. I would often have opportunity to pray for my family members, that they, too, would find this strength. But I would leave it at that.

"When I returned home I prayed that God would send 'someone' to my family to introduce them to Christ. I prayed that 'someone' would demonstrate and proclaim the gospel to them. After these prayers another crisis would arise and I would make the journey again to minister to the immediate need.

"My father's health was declining and the calls and visits became more routine. I was desperate for God to send 'someone' to my family, especially my dad. That was when I heard God say to me, 'I have been sending someone, Darryl. I have been sending you.' It was humbling. Through all of those prayers I didn't recognize God's answer."

God does not waste anything. He is the master of redemption. Even the failure to recognize the Spirit's leading in opportunities like this can be used to draw us to grow more sensitive and responsive. We are being invited to open our eyes and hearts, to pay attention to what God is doing and to recognize our part in this great work of grace.

Failure can provide an opportunity for reflection. Could our motives have been muddled? Is it time to sharpen our skills? Do we need to deepen our understanding of Scripture? Does a greater sensitivity to the Spirit need to be nurtured? These moments of pain and humiliation can be used by God to refine us. Rejection can inspire us to love as Christ loves. Fear can be transformed into bold determination. Missed opportunities can call us to intentional living and careful attention to the Holy Spirit. Failure is redeemable if we offer it to God for use in His transforming work.

Chapter *Seven*

Over and Over and Over

Time is precious. The investment of our time is the investment of our life. This gift from God has become a commodity in our culture to be portioned out according to the value of the opportunities available to us. Living intentionally for the cause of Christ can make a dramatic difference in the way we spend our time, especially when it comes to the people we spend it with. What we may have once considered an interruption in our carefully planned and prepared schedule can be seen as a precious opportunity to connect with someone far from God. We must invest intentionally and thoughtfully. But not sparingly. We have become cautious in our commitments and quick to push back when others seek a moment that we have reserved for ourselves. Opportunities to share the gospel are in some cases earned over time.

Bringing someone to faith in Christ is often a matter of cultivating trust and friendship. Developing relationships with those far from God requires patience and persistence. We will need to hear their stories and share our own. Our words will be tested, as will our character. Our lives will be examined. The invitation to follow Christ may need to be given over and over again.

The question may not be in the making of time for others but in the amount. When Isaiah had that glorious vision of God in the temple he was overwhelmed and quickly responded. When God asked, "Who shall I send, who will go for us?" Isaiah replied, "Here am I. Send me." With that God gave him his assignment to go and tell. Isaiah asked, "How long, O Lord?" In his answer, God didn't specify a length of time that would be required for this assignment. He only gave Isaiah an indication of when the mission would be complete. We may be eager to respond to the opportunities we have been given. Our hesitation to engage may be tied to a concern over the amount of time such engagement may cost us. Are we willing to invest until the mission is complete? Are we willing to love and serve and say something, over and over again?

In the stories that follow you will read of the intentional and lengthy investment of time in the people God has brought into the lives of these Christ-followers. They value the souls they have the privilege of connecting with by making the investment of time and prayer and love and friendship. Soul-winning is not an event, a moment. Soul-winning in these stories might be better defined as soul-loving. Though the amount of time invested isn't specifically defined, these relationships have taken years to develop and may take years yet before the decision to live for Christ is made. Time is precious. People are precious to God. What better investment than one that touches the heart of God? Our limited gift of hours and days, even years can impact eternity for those around us.

THE HANDLER

By Major Rob Lyle

My involvement with German Shepherd dogs allows me to interact with a variety of people—many who are far from God. Membership in the German Shepherd Dog Club of America and several regional clubs brings me into contact with new people on a regular basis. I have served as treasurer, recording secretary, and currently, president of the Northern New Jersey club. While this is an enjoyable hobby of mine, I am intentional about being available to witness and minister to those in the club.

Raising these dogs has become a family affair. Over the past twelve years, my son Jason has become one of the top breeders of German Shepherd dogs (GSDs) in the Northeast. He breeds and sells German Shepherd puppies and competitively shows them in American Kennel Club events. He has bred numerous champions. Normally, the owners of GSDs do not handle their own dogs in the show ring. This demands the hiring of a professional handler. We interviewed a number of reputable and experienced

German Shepherd aficionados, and that is how we met Frank Starr.[1] When Frank started handling German Shepherds for my son and me, our dogs were not of top show quality. But as our knowledge of the breed increased, informed decisions began to be made in Jason's breeding program, and our dogs started to win. My relationship with Frank began long before I had been exposed to Bill Hybels' book, *Just Walk Across the Room*. Hybels encourages Christians to take simple steps in pointing people to faith. At the core of this biblical approach is what Hybels describes as "Living in 3D." Living in 3D encourages Christians to reach out and interact with people who are already part of their social circle.

The simple components are outlined below:

- Develop friendships—by engaging in the lives of people around them
- Discover stories—before sharing their own story and God's redemptive story
- Discern next steps—by following the Holy Spirit's direction[2]

As the story of my relationship with Frank unfolds, I will meld this simple triad of steps into the narration.

Developing Friendships

Frank is middle-aged and married with two children who are both in college. He is a car salesman for a luxury car dealer in the Philadelphia area. Frank grew up with little exposure to church and the things of God. His wife, Rita, grew up in the Catholic Church. Currently, they are not churchgoers, although both are keenly aware of the existence of God and of spirituality.

Early on, my relationship with Frank was purely on a professional level. Yet as our time together increased and our dogs began to win, our friendship became more cordial. Frank has a natural tendency to show

---

[1]Names have been changed to protect the relationships.
[2]Hybels, Bill. *Just Walk Across the Room*. Grand Rapids: Zondervan, 2006.

dogs that have the greatest chance of winning. Frank loves a winner! Jason, Frank and I would often go out to dinner after a show. Our dinner conversations would center not only on German Shepherds, but on the stuff of life. I am constantly looking for an opportunity to divert the conversation from the "everyday" things of this life to life above.

I live a rather insulated life, as do many Christians. According to Hybels, "the longer a person attends church, the fewer evangelistic discussions they engage in with family and friends."[3] My tendency, as for most Christians, is to be what he calls a "cocooner"—someone who seldom ventures out of their cozy Christian circle.

One could say that our paths crossed coincidentally, but I believe that God brought Frank and me together for a purpose. As a follower of Christ, it is my duty to walk toward people who are far from God and to share the story of God's redemptive love. I see friends who are not Christ-followers through the eyes of Jesus and value them for the hidden potential inside them. God cares for them as people of value (see John 3:16), people He wants to restore and redeem. So I greatly appreciate Frank and value him as a human being with whom God desires to have a personal relationship. My first responsibility is simply to engage those who are far from God and to allow the Holy Spirit to aid me in developing friendships. Inevitably, some of these casual relationships will lead to closer friendships.

If not me, who? Might there be another Christian whom God would send to develop a friendship with Frank? Perhaps! In most instances, people need multiple encounters with Christians (often more than one person) to move them closer to a life-changing decision to follow Christ. But the truth is that God has chosen me! May I be fully attuned to the leadings of the Holy Spirit as I engage in the lives of people around me. And I challenge you to do the same.

Discovering Stories

In 2000, Frank operated a kennel in Rockland County, New York (approximately 15 minutes from my home). During this time, Frank stayed with the kennel owner, a mutual friend of ours. Frank has handled dogs for him

[3]Hybels, p. 61.

for many years. During this time, the three of us often met once a week to talk about German Shepherds, discuss our common interests and tell our life stories. Those encounters gave us an opportunity to drop the social personas that people tend to hide behind and to bond as true friends.

To move people closer to Christ, we must intentionally discover their stories. This requires that I speak less and listen more. In other words, my agenda must be an open book and I must allow my friend to share his story. As the friendship develops, I "earn the right" to hold deeper conversations about the other person's concerns, desires and dreams.

Doors of opportunity open as the Christian listens. Bonds of friendship and trust envelop the relationship as life experiences and challenges are shared. Hybels encourages Christ-followers to capitalize on these God-given opportunities. He says that "people living far from God need the redemption and strength and stability that you can offer—just as you did before you came to Christ."[4]

As Frank opened up to me in conversation, he shared that he and Rita were attending a Bible study on the book of Mark led by Rita's nephew, a born-again Christian. I encouraged him to try and apply the Scripture to his life, even in very minuscule ways. A few months later, I saw him at a dog show, where he rushed over to explain his change in behavior as a result of that suggestion. The night before he had gone out for dinner and stepped into the lounge for a drink before heading back to his hotel room. A hockey game was on television and a loud, over-zealous patron began to taunt him as he was cheering for the road team. Frank quickly removed himself from the situation, contrary to the way he typically would have reacted. Previously, he would have answered with a right and then a left! Frank credits his response with an increased desire to keep the peace and show respect for others—all a by-product of meditating on his Bible study lessons.

Our friendship might have ended abruptly if I had criticized Frank's lifestyle and dictated exactly how to embrace a life-changing relationship with Christ. But as we continue to talk, he is moving closer to Christ. Is he coming to faith in Christ as quickly as I would like? No, but he is reading his Bible and the Holy Spirit is beginning to convict him about specific

---

[4]Hybels, p. 89.

behavior. Frank freely shares small steps forward as well as his failures and shortcomings.

This type of relationship is risky! Christ-followers are to engage in the lives of people around them. They are to stay open-minded and listen to the life stories of their friends. Christ-followers are to pray for the opportunity to engage in spiritual discussions with their friends.

Discerning Next Steps

A critical next step is to listen to the prompting of the Holy Spirit and then act on the Spirit's guidance. Hybels encourages Christ-followers to "try to catch crystal-clear signals people send—often unintentionally—that inform you about their needs and that can guide you toward right resources to suggest."[5]

The Holy Spirit has led me to provide Frank and Rita with Bibles, an easy to read commentary on the book of Mark, the Bible on CD and several spiritual formation books. The Christ-follower can easily become a resource person for friends who are moving closer to Christ. In this role there is a chance to discern an opportune word and to ask good questions. A resource person also perceives practical needs and engages in small acts of thoughtfulness.

God has placed in my path a number of people, including Frank, who are far from Christ. I often wonder; "Why me, Lord? Isn't there someone else who could do a better job than I?" The reply is normally, "Get close to those I send your way!"

My prayer is that I might in some small way be used of God to influence others for Him. May I seek people out and point them to Christ! May I never give up! Frank has not yet made a decision to accept Christ as his Savior, but I will not give up! I will continue to pray! I will continue to follow the promptings of the Holy Spirit!

> "You are the salt of the earth. But if the salt loses its saltiness, how can it be made salty again? It is no longer good for anything, except to be thrown out and trampled underfoot" (Matthew 5:13).

---

[5]Hybels, p. 96.

FROM GARAGE SALE TO GLORY

By Captain Sujung Na

I decided to hold a garage sale one year. Many of our neighbors came and had a good time. One Asian girl seemed to enjoy the sale a lot. I learned that she had just moved to the United States and sensed that she was very lonely. She was very pleased to find someone who could speak in her mother tongue.

I invited her to the corps and she began attending happily. She had attended a while when my husband tried to give her an invitation to accept Jesus. She became totally and unpredictably upset. After this she no longer attended the corps. Her strong rejection was a shock to me.

This new friend was important to me. I wanted to keep the relationship with her, letting her know that I valued her. I didn't want to lose her. I spent a lot of time with her, calling her, taking her to lunch, etc. When she had her first baby I even went into the labor room with her. But during those times I never mentioned church or asked her to return. I wanted her to know that she didn't owe me anything. When I was with her, she would sometimes ask, "I don't even go to your corps. Why are you so nice to me?" I told her, "Because we are friends," even though my heart was saying, "Because I want you to accept Jesus and know Him." I invested more than two years in this friendship and almost gave up on her.

One day, after all of this time and patience, she sent me a letter. The letter indicated her deepest appreciation for my kindness and her reason for being so resentful of Christianity. Her older brother had joined a cult that identified itself as Christian and then committed suicide. She wrote about her unforgettable trauma in the letter. This sad memory of her brother haunted her for a long time, and she became resentful toward Christianity. It took years, but she had finally opened up and shared her story. I was glad I didn't give up on her.

Our relationship continued even though it was not as close as it had been. One day I felt the prompting of the Holy Spirit to speak to her again. I asked her to come to church and accept Jesus. Her answer was "no." Then one evening I got a call from her. She and her husband had decided to attend the corps the next Sunday. Her husband had been in a car accident, and she thought it was time to accept Jesus and attend church. She decided to attend The Salvation Army corps where an officer has developed a relationship with her.

She accepted Jesus as her Savior and is living as a disciple of Jesus now. Praise the Lord! God taught me from this experience the importance of living a 3D life—Developing Friendship, Discovering Stories, and Discerning Next Steps.

How long, O Lord, will we be privileged to walk with those who are far from God? We may not have years to spend with people. Sometimes we will have only a few minutes in the elevator or check-out line. But when we are given the opportunity to intentionally invest in friendship with those far from God, our time is a gift of value and love. Patience will be required as will our diligence to keeping their salvation our hope and goal. Our genuine interest, sensitivity and care will engender friendship with others that can lead them to friendship with Jesus. Evangelism will cost us something, but what better way to invest? Let us then invest in the lives of those around us for eternity!

Chapter *Eight*

In the Most Unlikely Places

S ometimes the presentation of the gospel can appear inconvenient. We might be most comfortable with people coming into our corps buildings asking us how to come to faith in Christ. In the safety and comfort of the corps we have everything we need to aid with a sinner being "born again." The birthing room could be either the Mercy Seat in the sanctuary or the corps library stocked with Bibles and books of theology, which should provide all answers to any questions. Usually a trained spiritual obstetrician (corps officer) is nearby and all should go smoothly. Many, if not most times, the proclamation of the gospel requires us to take it to the streets—and not always to the main street or side street, but sometimes to the alley ways and some of the most unlikely places. Such was the case with Major Jim Gingrich as he went beyond walking across the room to walking across the parking lot landing at a dumpster.

In 1994, Major Gingrich's devotion to evangelism took him from the Springfield, Ohio, corps out into the community, where he held summer open-air meetings for children in an elementary school parking lot. After witnessing these open-airs for a summer, the school principal decided to invite them indoors under the name of "Sonshine Club." These were one-hour weekly meetings involving 40–50 children. The following year a total of three schools were hosting Sonshine Clubs, and by 1999 this program had grown to include 13 elementary schools, five middle schools and three high schools with a total of 450 students enrolled! Chaplains were hired to assist in the Bible programs and the government-funding agency gave them the title of "Community Connectors"—a title that could be given to any and all who attempt to bring Christ to a dying world.

One day, as Major Gingrich was driving by one of these host elementary schools, he witnessed three small boys playing in the dumpster beside the school. He immediately recognized them as being from the Sonshine Club, so he pulled into the school and walked across the parking lot intending to chastise them for the dangerous situation in which they placed themselves. Before he could say anything he noticed one of the boys had pulled some food out of the dumpster and was eating it. The other boys quickly told him they were not playing in the dumpsters. They were starving and their mother told them they would have to go looking in the dumpsters to find something to eat. And they did. Their actions and their mother's advice caused the Major to reply, "Let me take you home. We need to talk."

On the way to their home Major Gingrich anticipated he would find a living situation which probably was not even as healthy as dining out of a dumpster. As he pulled up to the house, Mom was there on the front porch in a broken condition, which mirrored the broken condition of the house. She was almost completely passed out while still barely grasping on to her crack pipe. The front door to the house was wide open and revealed a lifestyle that was a threat to safety, security and sanity. It would take several days of work to bring this domicile up to the status of deplorable.

For the sake of Mom's rehabilitation and the safety of the children, the county Department of Human Services intervened and the three boys were placed in foster care. God's intervention was evidenced when all three boys were placed in foster care with a foster family who attended the Springfield corps! For the next several years Major Jim Gingrich and the entire corps family were able to see these boys come to faith in Christ and grow in grace.

Major Gingrich's own words bring to completion the story of saying something to someone about the Christ of redemption.

"In 2008, I sat in the auditorium for our daughter's high school graduation and couldn't stop the tears from flowing. Not really because of my daughter, although I was very proud of her. No . . . in the same graduating class, just a few names after my daughter's was read, was one of the brothers. He was a high school graduate and going to college in the fall on a full scholarship. All I could see was the sweet innocent child who was so hungry he was 'dumpster diving' living in a home only fit for roaches and rats—his life will never be the same . . . because of a walk across the parking lot."

PARKING LOT EVANGELISM

By Lieutenant Brett Cundiff

It is estimated that in the United States alone there are approximately 800 million parking spots. Parking spots are a requirement to new construction and most municipalities establish a minimum number needed based on the square footage and the occupancy of buildings. Most Salvation Army centers have them very close to the building; some in front, behind, on the side, even under and over the structures! They are so common that we often take them for granted and fail to utilize them for more than what they are named for... parking. Lieutenant Brett Cundiff, corps officer of the Ashville, North Carolina corps describes how his parking lot became an unexpected vehicle of evangelism.

"Not long after we returned from the NSE in 2009, an opportunity came along for Rachel, a soldier, to become the receptionist at the Center of Hope here in Asheville, NC. This gave her the chance to interact with all those who come to us for assistance and shelter. Soon she knew each of them by name and noticed a need for daily prayer for all the passersby and shelter residents. She began an outside prayer circle in our front parking lot. On any given day you would find Rachel outside after 5:00 p.m., holding hands with anywhere from 20-30 people in a circle singing, testifying and praying for all those present. Among them would be prostitutes, homeless, addicts of all kinds and many others thrown away by society. All united in voice and spirit to praise, thank and petition our God for healing, blessing . . . and SALVATION! The plan of salvation was frequently presented in the midst of this group gathered for prayer.

"One who was saved was named Dean. Dean was wonderfully born again in Rachel's prayer circle. He testified in the prayer circle that he had given his heart to Christ one day while there. Though he was still homeless, he was on his way to full recovery and transitioning from a homeless to a productive life. Unfortunately, while crossing a road he was tragically killed in a terrible accident not long after he came to faith in Christ.

"What a comfort to know that Dean is now with the Lord in Heaven. All because of a beautiful chain of events that began in a wonderful place called Glen Eyrie in 2009 when a timid, shy soldier was given the training and confidence to just *say something.*'"

The Glen Eyrie grounds provide some of the most beautiful landscape and views one could imagine. The land is beautiful. The plants and flowers are gorgeous and the sky seems bluer and brighter. Many hikers make their way up the hiking trails in an effort to be alone with God and their own thoughts. Long time NSE faculty member, Paul Luhn, found himself in a most unlikely place to witness. It was a witness in the wilderness.

"I arrived at Glen Eyrie a few days before the rest of the seminar staff and settled in my room at the castle. On Thursday morning I awoke very early and the Lord prompted me to take a hike up to Dawson Trotman's gravesite. Dawson Trotman was the founder of Glen Eyrie Conference Center and is buried on the land he loved. I didn't really feel like taking a hike by myself, but decided to obey.

"It was a beautifully crisp morning and I could see my breath as I hiked up the trail. When I arrived at the grave no one was there and I found a scenic spot overlooking the castle to pray. I asked God to send someone my way to pray with. It wasn't long before I heard footfalls coming up the trail toward the grave. A middle-aged man approached the gravesite and sat down a short distance from me to pray. I didn't know him, but decided to pray for him as he had a troubled look about him.

"Then I heard the Holy Spirit say, 'Walk over to him.' A sudden small urge of panic set in and I did not want to comply, but again I obeyed. When I approached him he looked up at me and we started a conversation. I asked him if he was there to pray and he asked me the same question. But then he surprised me by asking, 'May I ask what you are praying about?' He informed me that he had asked God to send someone to him this morning to find some answers to difficulties he was facing.

"When I told him God sent me up here to pray for him he listened intently as I shared what God had laid on my heart. He left there with new answers and clarity about the direction he needed to take. I'm glad I obeyed the leading of the Holy Spirit to 'just walk across the grave' to meet a lonely soul and share good news with him!"

In John 4 we read of Jesus meeting a Samaritan woman at the well (Jacob's well) in Sychar and speaking of "living water." In Jesus' day the community well became the place to gather both water and conversation. A modern day equivalent might be a local Starbucks. People gather there for refreshments, but also it can be a place to say something about your faith. Such happened for Captain Vicky Esqueda from the Salvation Army corps in El Centro, California.

"I attended NSE in August 2012 and I work on making a conscience effort to 'Walk Across the Room' if not every day at least a few times a week. God has opened door after door for me without me even trying. He brings the hurting across my path daily. Just this morning my husband and I had the opportunity to lead a hurting young man to Christ while sitting outside of a Starbucks having a meeting. We were busy answering our phones during this meeting and praying for those who were calling. We were not paying attention to anyone around us but were just going about our daily schedule.

"A young man approached us with his two adorable puppies which opened up a simple loving conversation on how important our dogs are to us. He had seen us praying several times, knew we were people of faith and was asking many theological questions he had had for years. He shared his personal story of trying out numerous churches, including the Jehovah Witnesses and the Unitarian Church, but still feeling empty. He admitted to being filled with anger, rage and bitterness, but he seemed to be a very gentle and sweet person on the outside. Little do we know what is going on in people's minds while they appear so 'normal.'

"As he repeated the sinner's prayer with us, the tears flowed as he released his anger and bitterness. It took several minutes as he stuck with it, cried through the pain, and then felt at peace. What is also amazing about this story is the whole time we talked, his puppies were jumping and playing, but during the time their owner was crying and praying, they lay quietly at his feet just watching him. My life has been touched and enriched by this morning's 'God appointed meeting.'"

In the Most Unlikely Places

Just where He needs me, my Lord has placed me,
Just where He needs me, there would I be.
And since He found me, by love He's bound me
To serve Him joyfully.

Mariam M. Richards
SA Songbook #706

Appendix A

What Others Have Said

QUOTES AND POEMS

"William Booth once explained that the church bell, pleasant sound that it was, said 'Come!'—but the Army's big bass drum on the street pounded out the exhortation, 'Fetch them!'

Shaw Clifton, Who Are These Salvationists?

"I want to tell what God has done through Christ, His well beloved Son, How my poor heart He sought and won, Can you wonder that I want to tell it?
I want to tell what God can do for sinners lost like me and you, Of sins washed white and garments new—can you wonder that I want to tell it?

I want to tell you what the Lord has done, what the Lord has done for me; He lifted me from the miry clay—Oh, what a happy day!
I want to tell you what the Lord can do, what the Lord can do for you; He can take your life as He did mine and make it brand new!"

Sidney Cox (Salvation Army Songbook #335)

"Christianity spread rapidly during the first century because all Christians saw themselves as responsible for disseminating the gospel."

Erwin W. Lutzer

What Others Have Said

"God is not saving the world; that is done.
Our business is to get men and women to realize it."

Oswald Chambers (1874–1917)

"If you want your neighbor to know what Christ will do for him, let the neighbor see what Christ has done for you."

Henry Ward Beecher (1813–1897)

"I look upon all the world as my parish."

John Wesley (1703–1791)

"If I thought I could save one more soul to the Lord by walking on my head and playing the tambourine with my toes, I'd learn how!"

William Booth (1829–1912)

"Evangelism isn't just something you 'do—out there'—and then get back to normal living. Evangelism involves taking people seriously, getting across to their island of concerns and needs and then sharing Christ as Lord in the context of our natural living situations."

Rebecca Manley Pippert

"As soon as a man has found Christ, he begins to find others. I will not believe that you have tasted of the honey of the gospel if you can eat it all yourself. When Andrew found Christ, he went to find his brother. He little imagined how eminent Simon would become! Simon Peter was worth ten Andrews, so far as we can gather from sacred history, and yet Andrew was instrumental in bringing him to Jesus. You may but speak a word to a child, and in that child there may be slumbering a noble heart which shall stir the Christian church in years to come. Andrew had only two talents, but he finds Peter. Go thou and do likewise."

Charles Spurgeon (1834–1892)

"Be to the world a sign that while we, as Christians, do not have all the answers, we do know and care about the questions."

Billy Graham

"Catch on fire with passion and people will come to watch you burn."
John Wesley (1703–1791)

"Here is the principle—adapt your measures to the necessity of the people to whom you minister. You are to take the Gospel to them with such modes and circumstances as will gain for it from them a hearing."
Catherine Booth (1829–1890)

"The minister lives behind a 'stained-glass curtain.' The layman has opportunities for evangelism which a minister will never have."
James McCord

"The people of Jesus' day thought holy men were unapproachable. But Jesus' work was in the marketplace. He made people feel welcome and that they had a place. His life was a constant demonstration that there were only two things that really mattered in this life—God and people. They were the only things that lasted forever."
Rebecca Manley Pippert

"The salvation of a single soul is more important than the production or preservation of all the epics and tragedies of the world."
C. S. Lewis (1898–1963)

"The church is under orders. Evangelistic inactivity is disobedience."
John R. W. Stott (1921–2011)

"The Christian is called upon to be the partner of God in the work of the conversion of men."
William Barclay (1907–1978)

"Taking the gospel to people wherever they are—death row, the ghetto, or next door—is frontline evangelism. Frontline love. It is our one hope for breaking down barriers and for restoring the sense of community, of caring for one another that our decadent, impersonalized culture has sucked out of us."
Charles Colson (1931–2012)

What Others Have Said

"You may not be able to put two sentences together of the Queen's English, but if you can say that you have been born again, if you can say, 'Once I was blind but now I see,' you will do for The Salvation Army!"

Catherine Booth (1829–1890)

"Men look for better methods, but God looks for better men."

Erwin W. Lutzer

"Witnessing is not spare-time occupation or a once-a-week activity. It must be a quality of life. You don't go out witnessing, you are a witness."

Dan Greene

Forgive Me God, I Had No Time

The year slipped by and time was spent,
And all the good things that I meant
To do were left undone because . . .
I had no time to stop and pause;
But rushed about, went here and there,
Did this and that, was everywhere.
I had no time to meditate
On things worthwhile. No time to wait
Upon the Lord and hear Him say,
"Well done, My child, you have shown the way."
And so I wonder, after all,
When life is o'er and I am called
To meet my Savior in the sky,
Where saints live on and never die,
If I can find one soul I have won
To Christ by some small deed I have done.
Or will I hang my head and whine,
"Forgive me, God, I had no time"?

A Treasury of Biblical Illustrations

"You never know till you try to reach them how accessible men are; but you must approach each man by the right door."

Henry Ward Beecher (1813–1887)

"Being an extrovert isn't essential to evangelism—obedience and love are."

Rebecca Manley Pippert

"Evangelism is a cross in the heart of God."

Leighton Ford

"Nothing will convince and convict those around us like the peaceful and positive way you and I respond to our twentieth century hurts and distress. The unbelieving world—your neighbors, the guy at the gas station, the postman, the lady at the cleaners, your boss at work—is observing the way we undergo our trials."

Joni Eareckson Tada

"Go for souls. Go straight for souls and go for the worst."

William Booth (1829–1912)

"Our task is to live our personal communion with Christ with such intensity as to make it contagious."

Paul Tournier (1898–1986)

"People say that it is hard to bring Jesus Christ and present Him before the lives of men today. Of course it is—it is so hard that it is impossible except by the power of the indwelling Holy Ghost."

Oswald Chambers (1874–1917)

"The disciples' decision to obey Jesus after the ascension—to go and make disciples—proved to be a pivot point in history. The world was never the same again."

Charles Colson (1931–2012)

"We're going to fill, fill, fill the world with glory; We're going to smile, smile, smile and not frown.
We're going to sing, sing, sing the gospel story; We're going to turn the world upside down."

John Larsson (Salvation Army Songbook #801)

What Others Have Said

"It is the duty of every Christian to be Christ to his world."

Martin Luther (1483–1546)

"The Great Commission is not an option to be considered; it is a command to be obeyed."

Hudson Taylor (1832–1905)

"He is not seeking a powerful people to represent Him. Rather, He looks for those who are weak, foolish, despised and written off and He inhabits them with His own strength."

Graham Cooke

"Great opportunities to help others seldom come, but small ones surround us daily."

Sally Koch

"Evangelism is a process of bringing the gospel to people where they are, not where you would like them to be. When the gospel reaches a people where they are, their response to the gospel is the church in a new place."

Vincent Donovan

"The world for God, the world for God, I give my heart—I'll do my part."

Evangeline Booth (1865–1950)

They thanked me for the words I spoke—
as if I could by any word of mine do any good!
As if the thought that healed came from my mind!
I know they only wanted to be kind—
but they should know the message isn't mine.
The word that heals just has to be Divine.
And any truth they recognize as true,
Though I may speak— it comes of course from You!

John Gowans (1934–2012)

"The scriptures begin by telling of a world that is without form, empty and in sheer chaos. God enters into this utter confusion and proclaims, 'Let there be light.' These four words jumpstart an entirely new reality that brings shape, life and order to the chaos. That is the great power of the spoken word. It can inspire, give courage, rescue, redeem and bring order to any context. Words can propel us forward, but we must start by being courageous enough to say something."

Steve Carter
Director of Evangelism
Willow Creek Community Church

"Lord, to whom shall we go? You have the words of eternal life." John 6:68

REFLECTIONS

The Salvation Army is the product of the faithful work and ministry of an evangelist. William Booth, who founded The Salvation Army, was not only a great social reformer and leader, but he was an evangelist.

I have a deep admiration and affection for The Salvation Army and am grateful for all that its people have meant to our ministry around the world. We can always count on you all to pray and work alongside us in our evangelistic Crusades, including our most recent major evangelistic outreach with "My Hope America."

Billy Graham

Over the years, it has been a real highlight to see these brothers and sisters [Salvationists] head out for their days of evangelism. The stories they bring back demonstrate their passion, obedience and lifestyle commitment to sharing the good news of Jesus Christ. Their lives model care, love and concern for those who do not yet understood what "new life" can be and set a high-bar example for followers of Jesus to follow. It has been a privilege to host them here at Glen Eyrie!

Jack McQueeney
The Navigators
Executive Director,
Glen Eyrie Conference Center

What Others Have Said

It never ceases to amaze me how this seminar changes the lives of people. I brought a corps member with me and, throughout the week, was privileged to see her change. She became so on fire for God that she was almost a different person.

She came back to the corps excitedly telling of her experiences with God in evangelism. I am resolved to encourage attendance, not only of my soldiers, but to guide other officers to take advantage of this opportunity as well. I think every corps across the nation should be utilizing this amazing God-filled week for their soldiers.

Linda McCormick, Lieutenant
Fergus Falls, MN

Going to the seminar changed my whole point of view in life. It made me realize how much people just want someone to listen. The stories touched my heart and made me realize that we have so many suffering people out there, not just the homeless or the drug addict. It could be anyone. I am blessed to be a soldier for The Salvation Army and to be able to give back what was freely given to me, by walking across the room.

Yolanda Recania, Recruiting Sergeant
Salvation Army Kroc Corps, San Francisco, CA

My husband and I participated in the 2011 National Seminar on Evangelism. We have since taken active roles in ministry, but we wouldn't have been used at this level if we hadn't participated in that seminar. I have always loved the Lord, and although I was an active member of the church and had served as a Sunday School teacher, I was terrified of approaching someone to tell them about God's love. I thought it would take a special talent. The seminar taught me volumes in practical and ordinary opportunities to witness for God.

Elizabeth Aranguren
DeSoto, TX

What I learned from the NSE sessions reinforced that I don't need to fix everything all at once. I can be present with people, even those with whom

SAYSOMETHING

I have severe disagreements. I believe that Jesus and the Holy Spirit are with me and will lead me to do or say whatever they want.

John Bennett, Major
Colorado Springs, CO

My husband and I have always said that NSE is like a "Brengle" for soldiers. It is such a privilege to attend the national conference, as it broadens a soldier's view of The Salvation Army, offers a vision for evangelism, provides tools to increase comfort in sharing, and makes it possible to have life-long friendships. It is definitely a mountaintop experience in so many ways and allows everyone to experience God more deeply and personally.

Darlene Harvey, Major
Chicago, IL

The awareness of peace and the presence of God so permeates the grounds of Glen Eyrie. Tucked away within the valley of large rocks, boulders and huge rimrocks are the kept secrets of people who have prayed and met with God. The experiences encourage seeking His counsel and walking the paths with other soldiers along this journey of faith. This is a special place of learning, seeking, and telling the story of Jesus.

You learn the importance of knowing your story with God. You have the opportunity to share that story with others and listen to their stories, too. As you listen to others share, your heart is opened to the beauty of a newly discovered relationship with Christ. The beauty of the Holy Spirit indwelling the lives of those at Glen Eyrie is most profound. You gotta go!

Steve and Janet Knapp
Dallas, TX

I find one of the biggest challenges for delegates is how to initiate conversation. I instruct my small group members to speak to a basic human need. In The Salvation Army we are pretty adept at recognizing physical need, but I encourage them to remember the needs people have to be noticed, to be appreciated and to be useful. These needs are universal and often open doors to speak to spiritual needs.

Sherrie Trucker
Roseville, MN

What Others Have Said

GLOOOOOORY!

Tony Lewis, Envoy
Philadelphia, PA

We need to be so careful in our relationships—to know when to speak and when to be quiet, to ensure we know the facts, and to speak when the Spirit prompts. How many people are lost because of a wrong word? How many people are encouraged by our edification? Do we really care?

A recent survey suggests that churchgoers only actually love 25% of their fellow congregants! How then, can we step further and evangelize? The NSE is a logical, systematic, communicative way to address these questions. Delegates consistently indicate success and highlight the NSE package as a mountaintop spiritual journey that envelops quality. Quality first, with quantity to follow naturally.

Carl Darby
Los Angeles, CA

I've learned that I must be attentive to the direction and timing of the Holy Spirit. It may be that all He is calling me to do is to befriend someone, or to plant a seed. Someone else may be called upon to nurture that seed and see it bloom in the Kingdom of God. I just need to be obedient to the leading of the Holy Spirit.

Pat Kukuc
Chicago, IL

To participate in the first National Seminar on Evangelism was and remains one of the most fulfilling experiences of our officership. The whole concept was truly inspired by the Holy Spirit. After nearly 44 years of effective ministry, it carries my wholehearted endorsement . . . May God's blessing continue to be upon the Seminar as it seeks to equip God's people to go out and "Walk Across The Room" to share Christ with others.

General Bramwell Tillsley

Appendix B

The Founder's Messages to Soldiers

The "Messages" or Letters printed on the following pages were written in 1907-08 by our beloved FOUNDER to the Soldiers of The Salvation Army.

SPEAKING FOR CHRIST

I

COMRADES AND FRIENDS,—There are a great many people on the earth, and a growing number in Heaven, who have been converted through some personal word spoken by the lovers of Jesus at unexpected time and in unusual places.

The opportunities for this kind of usefulness are so numerous that they cannot be counted. They come to us everyday, and to most of us many times a day. But, alas! How often they come and go unnoted and un-improved! This should not be. I want to ask you to take advantage of them.

I want you to feel that if you wear our blessed Uniform, or in any other way signify that you belong to The Army, people expect you to **say something** to them about eternal things.

In many cases your neglect of what appears to be a duty may cause some surprise, and even lead those who witness it to set you down as insincere, or as only half believing the great truths on such The Army lays so great a stress.

Of course, opportunities will ever be occurring to you to speak to the members of your own family about their spiritual interests. But it is not those opportunities to which, at this moment, I refer, important as they may be. I am asking you to avail yourselves of every chance of speaking to your Comrades on these subjects. I am asking for something more than this. I am urging you to seize every opportunity of putting in your word for Salvation with the ungodly people around you.

I am not now asking you to visit them in their homes, or their sick beds, in the dinking saloons, in the workshops or elsewhere, although that is important—very important—and multitudes of your Comrades all over the world have been successful in such efforts. But I am asking you to drop a word, or have a little conversation with the people you meet in the train, or on the tram; that when you buy or sell, when you are at the mill, when you meet friends or strangers by the way, you should be ready to speak a word for God and Salvation.

Now some of you will say, "I cannot do that sort of thing. I never could. I do not like it." Perhaps not. But just wait a bit. I shall hope to show you not only that you *can* do this kind of work, but how you may find pleasure in doing it.

In order to do this, I recommend you to—

1. *Make up your mind to speak about God's will to the first stranger that crosses your path after reading this Message.*
Do not think it absolutely necessary to decide beforehand what you shall say. The Holy Spirit will supply you with words, and bless you in speaking.

2. *Keep a sharp look out for opportunities as they arise.*
Again, I say, God will guide you. But wherever there is a chance, strive to make the most of it. Oh, how often these chances come and go unimproved!

Do we not often reproach ourselves for having let such opportunities slip? "Why did I not speak about his soul to that man with whom I had the chat?" Or, "Why did I not drop a word to that woman whom I spoke to on some other matter?"

Sometimes those to who God has given us the chance of speaking are suddenly stricken down, and pass away. Then in bitterness of heart we say: "Oh, why did I not utter a word of warning when the

SAY SOMETHING

chance was mine? Now they are gone and beyond my reach forever!"
Perhaps God, on the Judgment Day, will echo that question, "Why?"
Therefore, be watchful.

3. In speaking to strangers, be careful not to give needless offence.
Speak kindly and gently, and with all due courtesy and respect, and
you will be surprised how far you can go without creating ill feeling.
Should anyone ever be offended, you must apologize.

4. Be sure and deal faithfully when you do speak.
In many cases you can create interest by relating something of your
own experience. Testimony is a wonderful thing, and, when given
modestly, with faith in God, generally moves the hearts of those who
hear it.

**5. Be sure every time, and all the time, to cast yourselves on God
for His blessing on what you say, remembering that He is with
you.**
Do not be discouraged if your words are rejected, or received with
scorn, or, it may even be, cast back in your teeth with sneers or curses.
You can remember that this was the experience of your Lord, and that
it is no proof that you have not said the right thing, and that it may
not have the desired effect.

It is not you who do the work, but the truth you speak. Unknown
to you, the leaven you have imparted may be working in the heart
you have approached, and the seed you have sown may be destined to
bring forth precious fruit.

For, soon or late, to all that sow,
The time of harvest shall be given;
The flower shall bloom, the fruit shall grow,
If not on earth, at last in Heaven!

My Comrades, let me ask whether you are in the habit of following
this method of usefulness? If you care, I congratulate you, and bless you in
the name of the Lord. Go on, and prosper more and more!

If it has not been your custom to speak for your Lord after this fashion, I want you to ask Him to forgive your neglect; to promise Him that you will do better in the future, and that you will begin today.

Your affectionate General,
WILLIAM BOOTH

SPEAKING FOR CHRIST

II

COMRADES AND FRIENDS,—I spoke to you last week about the duty of testifying to both friends and strangers of the value of Salvation, and the importance of engaging in the service of God.

Before I go further I want to remark that although many of our people experience difficulty and reluctance in testifying for Christ, we are no whit behind any other section of Christ's people. On the contrary, as is well known, no section of the community makes a bolder or more public confession of faith than does The Salvation Army. Ours is peculiarly a "house-top religion."

Still there is room for an immense advance even with Salvationists in the discharge of this duty. Let us therefore enlist a body of Soldiers who will accept it as a special obligation before God.

I. BUT NOW I WANT TO ASK, WHY THIS UNWILLINGNESS TO SPEAK UPON A SUBJECT OF SUCH THRILLING AND INFINITE IMPORTANCE, AFTER THE FASHION I HAVE DESCRIBED?

1. *Well, the first reason may be traced to custom.*
   Religious people do not generally discuss their religion in public; anyway, they do not very often describe their own experience. God and His services are, they consider, only to be referred to on particular occasions, and in what are called sacred places.

   To speak of the love of Christ, the value of the soul, the forgiveness of sins, and the hope of Heaven, in a railway carriage, or a goods store, or by the roadside, or at the tea-table, would be regarded by many professing Christian people as being bad form, if not next door to profanity.

2. *Another reason for this neglect can be traced to ignorance.*

Many Soldiers do not see it to be their duty to personally warn their friends and neighbors, or to invite them to the Cross.

Many Soldiers, I am sorry to say, do not see it to be their duty to save sinners at all! They think this is the work of their Officers; that is, of those who are set apart and paid for their performance of the task. They do not feel any responsibility for the souls of their workmates or the strangers about them, but seem willing to let them go, quietly and comfortably, down to Hell, so far as they are concerned. Much less would they run the risk of sacrificing their good opinion, or incurring their displeasure, by speaking to them in an omnibus, or the deck of a steamer, or in the roadway.

What an awful blindness this is! May God open the eyes of all such ignorant, shrinking souls who may be here today.

3. *Thoughtlessness is another reason why Soldiers fail to discharge this duty.*

The obligation to take advantage of the opportunity does not strike them at the moment.

Oh, how I have mourned on my own account over chances of this description lost for want of thought. "Why, "I have said to myself, "did it not occur to me to speak? *That* chance I can never have again, and I may never have another."

4. *Sometimes the reason may be traced to a spurious kindliness.*

There is a fear of hurting people's feelings. I am afraid that this fear often shuts the mouths of those who ought to utter words of solemn warning, and for this reason many a poor sinner is left to die in the dark.

And yet it is often a great mistake to suppose that testimony on the subject of religion is disagreeable; in many instances it would be most welcome, especially from the lips of a Salvationist.

5. *Alas! There is occasionally another reason, which is a very un-happy one. The Salvationist is troubled with doubts and fears about his own safety; and, not being certain about his own Salvation, is, consequently, unwilling to speak to others on the subject.*

Only too often this voice is silent because he is not sure about his own standing with God, and the rightness of his own life. It is true that the stranger by his side may know nothing of his inconsistency; but that friend, whose name is Conscience, who resides within him, knows how matters stand between him and God. And while he is saying to himself, "Shall I speak to this man about his soul, or invite him to our Meeting?" Conscience may be saying, "Would it not be best to get your own heart put right, before you begin to doctor other people?" "Physician, heal thyself."

6. *But, more commonly, this reluctance may be traced to a strange feeling of shame which arises when the duty of speaking to people about their souls presents itself.*

II. HERE LET ME OFFER TWO OR THREE SUGGESTIONS WHICH MAY HELP YOU TO MASTER THOSE FEELINGS.

1. *When you see your chance, take up your cross boldly, and go straight for the discharge of your duty.*

2. *Listen to no arguments in favor of silence from your own heart.*

Do not be hindered by what people may think or say about you. If you see the opportunity of warning a soul from the way of death, seize it there and then.

Beware of the dangerous notion that we are not to speak for Christ unless moved thereto by a Divine impulse.

John Wesley tells us that he was at one time so far influenced by this doctrine, that he resolved to give it a fair trial. Accordingly, he says he rode from York to Barnet without being moved to speak to a single soul. Then he threw this notion overboard, and began again to speak to all with whom he came in contact, whether he felt led to do so or not.

The opportunity for this or any other kind of usefulness is the Divine call.

3. *At the onset, always throw yourselves on God for His guidance and blessing on what you say and do.*
I have already said this, but I say it again.

4. *Reckon on the conscience of every individual to whom you speak being on your side.*
For, however worldly they may appear, or with whatever scorn or indifference they may at first receive your words, everyone has a conscience, although perhaps dormant, but which may be quickened by the Holy Spirit using some word you may say.

5. *Study how you can perform your task in the most effective manner.*
Treat all to whom you speak with kindness and reasonable respect.

6. *With a heart full of love, practice will bring the chief qualification for this kind of work; and that is courage.*
Practice, plenty of practice, still more practice will ultimately make you perfect.

Your affectionate General,
WILLIAM BOOTH

Epilogue

T his book, *Say Something*, is finished, but the mission has just started. This sin-sick world is in need of hearing the message of hope, but how will they hear if we don't say something?

You've read stories of evangelism successes, failures and the attempts in between. If your confidence in your abilities and skills is weak, there exist for you helps in various forms. First, turn to God in prayer and ask him how He would do your job if He were you. Second, consult your corps officer. Corps officers are trained and commissioned to make the salvation of souls their primary concern. Third, evangelism books, resources and seminars abound. In fact, the National Seminar on Evangelism provided the training and passion for those who have participated in the writing of this book.

Don't be discouraged if the results are not dramatically obvious. A clergyman was once asked by the Duke of Wellington, "How are you getting on with the propagation of the gospel abroad? Is there any chance of the Hindus becoming Christians?" To which the clergyman replied, "Oh no! I do not see anything doing there; I see no reason to suspect any work of the kind being successful." "Well," said the Duke, "what have you to do with that? What are your marching orders? Are they not 'Go ye into all the world, and preach the gospel to every creature'? (Mark 16:15). Do your duty, sir, and never mind results."

Let's take this advice to heart. Let's be willing to *Say Something*, and leave the results to God.

My Covenant

Having been a delegate to the NATIONAL SEMINAR ON EVANGELISM, attended the classes in training on evangelism, studied the biblical imperatives concerning evangelism, and practiced the art of personal evangelism, I now rededicate myself to God and promise that I will renew all my efforts from this time forward to seeking the salvation of the lost. I promise to take every opportunity given to me by God to communicate the good news of salvation through Christ and will let nothing deter me from my desire to win souls for Him. I do here and now make this covenant with God and do pray that He will, through the power of His Holy Spirit, enable me to keep the covenant as long as I shall live.

Signed this _____ day of _____,

In the year _____, at _____

_____
(Signature)

Crest Books

Salvation Army National Publications

Crest Books, a division of The Salvation Army's National Publications department, was established in 1997 so contemporary Salvationist voices could be captured and bound in enduring form for future generations, to serve as witnesses to the continuing force and mission of the Army.

Judith L. Brown and Christine Poff, eds., *No Longer Missing: Compelling True Stories from The Salvation Army's Missing Persons Ministry*

Terry Camsey, *Slightly Off Center! Growth Principles to Thaw Frozen Paradigms*

Marlene Chase, *Pictures from the Word; Beside Still Waters: Great Prayers of the Bible for Today; Our God Comes: And Will Not Be Silent*

John Cheydleur and Ed Forster, eds., *Every Sober Day Is a Miracle*

Helen Clifton, *From Her Heart: Selections from the Preaching and Teaching of Helen Clifton*

Shaw Clifton, *Never the Same Again: Encouragement for New and Not–So–New Christians; Who Are These Salvationists? An Analysis for the 21st Century; Selected Writings, Vol. 1: 1974-1999 and Vol. 2: 2000-2010*

Christmas Through the Years: A War Cry Treasury

Frank Duracher, *Smoky Mountain High*

Easter Through the Years: A War Cry Treasury

Ken Elliott, *The Girl Who Invaded America: The Odyssey Of Eliza Shirley*

Ed Forster, *101 Everyday Sayings From the Bible*

William Francis, *Celebrate the Feasts of the Lord: The Christian Heritage of the Sacred Jewish Festivals*

Henry Gariepy, *Israel L. Gaither: Man with a Mission; A Salvationist Treasury: 365 Devotional Meditations from the Classics to the Contemporary; Andy Miller: A Legend and a Legacy*

Henry Gariepy and Stephen Court, *Hallmarks of The Salvation Army*

Roger J. Green, *The Life & Ministry of William Booth* (with Abingdon Press, Nashville)

How I Met The Salvation Army

Carroll Ferguson Hunt, *If Two Shall Agree* (with Beacon Hill Press, Kansas City)

John C. Izzard, *Pen of Flame: The Life and Poetry of Catherine Baird*

David Laeger, *Shadow and Substance: The Tabernacle of the Human Heart*

John Larsson, *Saying Yes to Life*

Living Portraits Speaking Still: A Collection of Bible Studies

Philip Needham, *He Who Laughed First: Delighting in a Holy God*, (with Beacon Hill Press, Kansas City)

R.G. Moyles, *I Knew William Booth; Come Join Our Army; William Booth in America: Six Visits 1886 - 1907; Farewell to the Founder*

Quotes of the Past & Present

Lyell M. Rader, *Romance & Dynamite: Essays on Science & the Nature of Faith*

R. David Rightmire, *Sanctified Sanity: The Life and Teaching of Samuel Logan Brengle*

Allen Satterlee, *Turning Points: How The Salvation Army Found a Different Path; Determined to Conquer: The History of The Salvation Army Caribbean Territory*

Harry Williams, *An Army Needs An Ambulance Corps: A History of The Salvation Army's Medical Services*

A. Kenneth Wilson, *Fractured Parables: And Other Tales to Lighten the Heart and Quicken the Spirit; The First Dysfunctional Family: A Modern Guide to the Book of Genesis, It Seemed Like a Good Idea at the Time: Some of the Best and Worst Decisions in the Bible*

A Word in Season: A Collection of Short Stories

Check Yee, *Good Morning China*

Chick Yuill, *Leadership on the Axis of Change*